BEIRUT
diary

Rev. Charles L. Breindel

CL Breindel LLC
Danville, Virginia

Beirut Diary
All rights reserved. Copyright CL Breindel LLC, 2005

ISBN 0-9767549-1-6

Library of Congress Control Number: 2005905298

Printed in the United States of America

Book Design: Lisa R. Gray

Author Contact Information:
Rev. Charles L. Breindel
154 College Avenue
Danville, Virginia 24541-3708 USA
434/792-9456
frcharles@adelphia.net

*Dedicated to Charlotte and Jerome
who nurtured me in faith in my God and myself*

Special thanks to my English teacher brother
Joseph J. Breindel and to Pamela Riedel, Ed.D.,
Professor at Averett University, for their reading,
rereading, and editing talents.

Table of Contents

Preface v

Introduction 1

 Original Title Page (1983) 5

 Original Introduction (1983) 6

 Original Preface 9

The Diary 15

 Original Epilogue (1983) 147

Epilogue 155

Correspondence and Other Referenced Materials,
Back Home in the USA 161

Where Are They Now? 185

PREFACE

This book has been a long time in formulation. It has been an idea gestating in my mind and in those of many dear friends who wanted to hear the story of my third and final trip to the American University of Beirut. It was well known by many that I kept detailed diaries during those early days of international travel. Because of that, many have been requesting the publication of the diary from that fateful trip 23 years ago. But I was not ready to share my story, nor the significance that those days in Beirut in the spring of 1982 had on my life. I was still an "open book," naive and looking for meaning in life, after I got back home. What I found in Beirut was not apparent to me until many years later when good hindsight brought into better perspective the life-changing experience of Beirut.

I went to Beirut as a young visiting assistant professor to teach a short course in health planning. I returned still the same professional, but with a different worldview, a budding sense of God in my life, and a new hunger for understanding and wisdom that was unparalleled in my prior life. Before Beirut, I was "putting in time," existing, not being particularly satisfied, yet not dissatisfied. Not knowing the possibilities available in my life, I was unaware that there were other possibilities, other realities.

After Beirut, I was alive with feelings, emotions, and ideas, all sorts of questions about who I was, what I was, and why I existed. I came home from Beirut fully aware that I had an agenda to live out, a purpose as-yet unrevealed to me in my living. I was compelled to begin a search for my role and purpose in life. What began as a question: "Why did I have this amazing experience in Beirut?" soon became "What am I supposed to do with my life, having experienced the invasion of Lebanon, capture, fear, death, and joyful salvation?"

The winter after I returned from Beirut, I typed up an edited version of my diary, gave it a catchy title "An Expendable Commodity," and shared it with several publishing houses, and some friends. It was too close to the events which were recorded there to have meaning. The story in the diary was still in its early stages of unfolding. My part of the bigger story was not yet completed, so I put the book away for the time, knowing that there would be no interest without knowledge of the bigger story of the Middle East conflict.

Now there is fuller knowledge of the roles of the major actors in the Middle East. There have been other wars besides the one I survived there. American involvement there is critical and an intrinsic part of American international policy. Many want to learn more about the Middle East, the experience of war there and the happiness of survival. The time for sharing my story in the diary has arrived.

What follows is a story, told through a private diary, never originally intended for public reading. It is that hastily typed copy of the diary from the winter of 1982-83 which forms the body of this book. It is interspersed with personal correspondence to and from me, some later stories written about my trip to Beirut, a few newspaper clippings, and related documents. (These insertions to the original diary appear in italics.)

It is a very simple story. It is about a man with a newly heightened spiritual awareness caught unexpectedly in a war. Thus, it is a biography of an unimportant person in an important time and place. It is a tale about his ability to experience the war, to hear the people and feel the events of war. In that sense it is a bird's-eye view of a war from one perspective. It is about finding faith in God and self so deeply that life was changed completely, and a new search for God and meaning began. In that sense it is a religious story.

The full meaning of the story of hostages, war, terror, and daily living in the Middle East (whether Lebanon, Israel, Palestine, Jordan, Kuwait, Saudi Arabia, Iran, or Iraq, to name subsequent countries of war and terror) can now be understood. So this story can be told and perhaps understood, or at least appreciated, by many.

The full meaning of my life, the life of the diary writer, is now better understood. The new journey which Beirut began has unfolded. So the personal interpretation of the experiences of Beirut by that young professor is now evident.

I am the writer of the diary, the writer of some of the letters, and the recipient of the other letters. I am the young naive professor who got caught in a war, panicked, died to self, and began to grow. I am now the Roman Catholic priest and pastor of a parish church and school. I am one who found God in 1982 in war-ravaged Beirut.

I hope that those who read this little book will find encouragement in this short story. Most people move along in life with no necessity to examine their raison d'etre, and how God calls them to fulfill it. I needed to be stopped dead in my tracks before I would allow myself to question, to doubt and eventually to grow. For me it took a war and thousands of deaths before I accepted that I was naive, that I was not living the life and fulfilling the potential for which my Creator made me. I share this story in the hope that others will find it a gentler and safer "baseball bat" for reflection.

Rev. Charles L. Breindel
Danville, Virginia
December 2005

INTRODUCTION

The basis of this book is a diary that I wrote on my journey to Lebanon in May and June 1982. It has been edited to remove some very personal or extraneous information. Most personal information, however, remains. The edited diary, with its original title page and introduction follow. It was first prepared about January 1983.

The diary occasionally refers to letters written and received, telexes, newspaper items, and other material. I have included these materials within the body of the diary, but set in italics. One can ignore these extra items and read only the diary. However, I believe that these additional materials will help to understand the intensity of the unfolding drama, even though they may not contribute much additional information.

In preparing the diary for sharing, after having put it away in the attic for more than two decades, I was quite struck by several things when I read it. I remembered many things from those stressful days in Beirut which were not found in the diary. Other events were included but were not recorded as I remembered them. There were events that I recorded as if they were simply normal events in an otherwise inconsequential day. One such example is my encounter with Jerius Khuri on two occasions, one of which was an intense discussion of God and the meaning of faith. In my memory the blind man Jerius was quite angry at God for his condition of blindness and resented my discussion of God. In the diary which I recorded, there are two meetings with the blind man, but neither expresses the intensity which I felt. Why? I think the answer may be related to my refusal to deal with difficult matters when there were more pressing concerns - war and survival - in the front of my mind.

Similarly, I came home in awe of the experience I had while running on the oval track of the green field on Friday morning June 3. I was sure that I heard a voice speaking to me about imminent danger. It nearly obsessed me at first. Yet, in my diary (and two letters) I mention it either as a "feeling" or as a mere sense of foreboding. I believe my refusal to admit the depth of my experience was due to my inability to fathom it and then deal with its meaning. I made light of it and then ignored it, even though I could not do that for very long.

Reading the diary these many years later, I am also struck by the clarity of the danger in which I was living. Despite my regular reminders to myself that "everything was okay," and that there was no great danger around me, it was not true. What I was really recording was not the truth of a safe situation but my strong desire - my great need to believe - that all was well and that danger was not just around the corner. Because of this, I think even the casual reader of the diary will experience a sense of foreboding danger as the diary unfolds. What was, for me, a mechanism to cope with the growing difficult situation in Beirut by telling myself over and over that there was no danger has, in hindsight, the effect of making it very clear that things were getting "hot," and that something bad was going to happen. As I read it to prepare for this little book, it was like watching a Hitchcock film in which little clues build toward an eruption of fear and terror.

Finally, the rereading of the diary made clear for me that the basis for my change of life from professor to priest, many years later, had its foundation and roots in the dramatic events of Beirut, Lebanon, in May and June of 1982. The days in Beirut, primed by a religious retreat on the front end, brought me in touch with myself in a new and wonderful way. My life began to change during those twenty-five days. Upon returning home, the changes were irreversible. The roots of my vocation as a Roman Catholic priest can be traced directly to Beirut. It was there I first experienced God speaking to me. It was there I first recognized God speaking to me. It was there I first listened to God and obeyed, and, more important, trusted. In Beirut I lost all my self-reliance and had no one to depend upon but God. So I took the risk and did it. And I found that it worked. And it was in Beirut that June that I let God use my mind, and my hands, and my voice, and my heart to serve others. I never knew that God would accept the offer of someone like me for service to others. But I gave myself to God, and God accepted the offer, and God helped people like Jerius and the others held captive, through my mind and heart and hands and voice. I could never forget that when I got home, and I wanted it to happen again. It was the beginning of my giving myself into His use.

Beirut in 1982 formed the very personal, intellectual and spiritual basis of my life from then on. I thank God for the gift of Beirut; I am sad only that so many others had to suffer so that I might grow and find myself. At least that is how I felt for years.

Maybe I have said enough. It may be time to read the diary. People have always told me that it would make a better movie than a book. But I would jokingly reply that Robert Redford and Richard Chamberlain were no longer available to play the title role of the tall blond professor. Maybe you'll wish it were a movie instead of a book. Whatever you wish, remember that it is a true story, at least as true and real as I can remember and retell. For me that is enough.

An Expendable Commodity:
An American in Beirut

Charles L. Breindel

1983

ORIGINAL INTRODUCTION

This is my own story. It is personal. It is a private story, full of my ideas, impressions and feelings. It is a true story to the best of my memory. The names of the people are real as are the places. It was recorded by me as a diary or personal journal. Its original purpose was to be a "running letter" to my family back in Virginia. Since communications were difficult by post or phone from Lebanon, I intended the diary to be one long letter home. When writing in the diary, I envisioned someone, mostly my family members, and wrote as if I were writing a note to them. In that sense, perhaps calling it a "diary" is misleading since diaries are typically not written with particular people in mind.

It is also a spiritual story because I am a spiritual person. Just before departing on the trip which is recorded in this diary, I had an experience of a deepening religious commitment in my own life. The events that unfolded during the twenty-five days of this story brought to life the spiritual parts of me and made me sensitive to a superhuman Actor in my life.

Finally, the story is one of deep emotions, from strong love and carefree joy, to fear and terror, and eventually to the numbing of my emotions as my coping with an untenable environment of war overwhelmed me.

In preparing this manuscript for others to read, I was hesitant to share my personal diary. I wrote this diary originally as a continuous letter to my family and not with any intentions for others to see it. It was my minute-by-minute record of thoughts and experiences, to be read and shared with family, that is, with dear ones who understood and accepted me and my personal quirks. The exposing of one of my "letters" to a public readership seemed unacceptable at first. However, I have exercised a small amount of editing of the original diary to make it more acceptable to my family and me for sharing, but the editing has been minimal. My family has read the manuscript and has approved its use for general distribution. I commend them for their kindness and support in this undertaking.

I wanted to give my story a clever title, one that was at once attractive to potential readers, yet clear and indicative of the contents of the book. Parodying Gershwin, I thought originally to call it "An American in Beirut." But cuteness seemed quite trite, considering the investment of feelings and effort that allowed for the generation of this diary. So I dismissed that title and selected instead a phrase that I had heard used to describe us Americans who got trapped in the western sector of Beirut in June 1982. I do not recall when I first heard it said of us, but the concept was good, correct, and all-too-clear; for when the U.S. Embassy evacuated at the onset of the war and left us alone and unadvised, we Americans knew that we were expendable commodities. [expendable: denoting supplies or equipment that can be sacrificed. Funk and Wagnells Standard Desk Dictionary, Volume 1. New York: 1979, p. 223.]

Flashbacks, unanticipated emotional reliving of past experiences, occurred for a time after my initial preparation of this manuscript. These made my life quite difficult and uncomfortable in the short term after my return to the United States. A counselor friend told me that flashbacks were necessary and wholesome after a traumatic experience. I could not deal with this diary and the emotional memories that it brought back for a long time. I say this to emphasize how difficult it was to commit to sharing this personal diary, so full of strong feelings and unspent emotions. Hopefully, with the completion of this project, a catharsis will have been achieved for me and I will again be free to go on.

Charles L. Breindel, January 1983

PREFACE

It was July already and I had been back from Beirut for about three-and-a-half weeks. But this was my first week back to work and I was not psyched for it at all. When my wife called to tell me that there was a free dress rehearsal of the Ice Follies that afternoon, I wasn't really interested. I was not interested in much of anything those days, not ice-skaters, not work, not much of anything but my four daughters. But I felt I would rather be bored with the family than bored alone at work, so I said I would meet them at the Richmond Coliseum for the 2:00 dress rehearsal.

It was 2:20 when the lights went out and the Coliseum was blackened for the beginning of the performance. With the darkness all around, I caught my breath. From out of nowhere and floating across the ice came the sound of a live orchestra. Drum rolls. A monotonous timpani. As I struggled for air, I began to feel a sense of terror. Then the lights came on slowly and, from somewhere far off in the heights of the Coliseum high above the ice, soft pinkish-red glowing lights began to move on the surface of the ice. The drum continued to pound and the red glow penetrated an otherwise blackened panorama. I sat all alone in the midst of that group of spectators sobbing. I never saw the figure skaters move out onto the ice and into the red glow because my eyes, along with my heart, were locked somewhere in West Beirut watching the sights of warfare in a night sky above the city. For me it was not July but early June. How could I tell my family beside me that, although I was sitting in the Coliseum in Richmond, somehow I was somewhere else too?

I felt that I was making an amazing readjustment after my dramatic experience of being caught in West Beirut and captured. I had taken a couple of weeks off, including five days of camping at the beach with the girls. I felt a bit guilty for causing them stress when I was apparently missing. I sometimes even felt a bit of anger at everyone who was over there and had allowed it all to happen. Mostly, however, I just felt strongly and prayed that somehow I could go back to May 22 and have another chance to make the decision about the trip and, in so doing, could choose not to go to Beirut.

Six days prior to the Ice Follies I was attending a social gathering of couples on a Sunday afternoon. The party was enlivened with the typical kinds of cocktail party conversation. I was not talking but was trying to listen to the myriad of chattering folks. The noise of the thunderstorm outside made it somewhat difficult for me to hear all of the conversations. In between the booms and claps of thunder, I focused on the lady who was telling about her dreams. She said something to me quite unexpected. I heard her clearly state that she envisioned in her dream that her husband went away on a business trip and he never returned. When she said that phrase "he never returned," I thought of myself, my family, and my recent trip to Beirut. The thunder booming did it to me then. I stood there in the middle of the party crying like a baby, quite confused at what was happening to me. For the moment I was completely unaware that I was reliving one of my many moments of fear that I had tucked away inside my head since Beirut.

When I accepted a visiting professorship at the American University of Beirut in early 1980, I could not have guessed that it would one day bring me into the throes of war and possible death. It was during my third visit to the American University of Beirut (AUB), the one from which I had just returned, that I recorded the diary which is the subject of this book.

I was 32 years old when I accepted the offer to be a visiting professor at AUB. At the time I was an assistant professor at the Medical College of Virginia, Virginia Commonwealth University, in Richmond, where I taught in a masters degree program in health administration. My background in public health policy and regional health planning in Pennsylvania, together with my Ph.D. in health administration and planning from Penn State, made me a quite good teacher and writer on planned change in health care, especially in rural and developing areas. It was no surprise then that I should one day be involved in teaching health services administration and health planning in a developing part of the world such as Lebanon. It was the same subject matter that I lived, worked, and taught here in the United States. That I wound up at AUB is simply a fluke, a function of the nationality of my first international student.

My first visit to teach at AUB in May 1980 was exciting, although the tension that I experienced due to my first exposure to gunfire and the reminiscence of a war-torn country were unsettling, yet maturing. But I was enthusiastic to return, as I was full of awe and wanderlust for the Middle East.

The second trip to the American University of Beirut occurred in the spring of 1981, but the political and military climate in Lebanon was so tense that the trip had to be canceled by the University. What the American papers called the "Zahle missile crisis" was the reason for the cancellation. My family and friends were nervous when I had considered going on the trip. They so often asked if I really had been planning to travel to a part of the world that was so dangerous.

I did return eventually, in March 1982, not to teach, but to work on a research project in health planning and policy analysis in Lebanon. I visited the University for about twelve days during which time I worked long days on a manuscript and research proposal, hopefully to be funded by the

Lebanese Ministry of Health. Also while there in March, I designed my graduate course for later in the year, met with my prospective medical students, and laid the detailed plans for my return in May to teach the course as scheduled.

There was much tension and a little bit of fighting while I was there, but it did not frighten me at all. The people were so kind, so gregarious, that I was not afraid. The civil strife, the fighting among the many factions in Beirut and Lebanon - all seemed to be very predictable and distant. There was much talk that Israel would one day take the southern part of Lebanon that spring. Indeed, the talk on the streets suggested that it would happen in the summer, just prior to the upcoming presidential election. My academic chairman there reminded me that this possible time of tension would occur after my May-June visit, so that I should still plan to come in these months without any fear of war or strife. If the street talk were true, he reminded me, I would be back home in the United States long before any fighting might possibly occur. We joked about that several times in March.

When I returned to the United States in mid-March I had a busy two months of work, family, and planning for my return to Beirut. It was also during this time that I went on a three-day religious retreat called a Curcillo weekend. The three days of reflection and study that I undertook had a dramatic effect in my life, my thinking, and my spirituality. Even though it was over a month after my Curcillo that I went to Beirut again, I was still deeply involved in the growth reverberations that had begun in me during that weekend. As a result, the diary that I wrote in Beirut in May and June is full of feelings which I had about God, myself and my heightened spirituality.

So now I turn to share with the reader the diary of those twenty-five days of my visit to Beirut, Lebanon and AUB in May and June of 1982.

Charles Breindel and his daughters,
just before going to Beirut the first time.

ITINERARY

Flight / Travel Schedule

May 22, 1982   Richmond, Virginia to Beirut, Lebanon via London
Drove to Dulles International Airport
Departed Dulles at 7:15 p.m.
Arrived Heathrow, London at 7:15 a.m. on May 23
Departed London at 10:30 a.m.
Arrived Beirut at 4:15 p.m.

June 10   Departed Beirut on Thursday, 1:00 p.m. for
Junieh, Lebanon

June 12   Departed Junieh on Saturday, 6:28 p.m. on the
S.S. Edy for Larnaca, Cyprus; seized by Israeli
navy at 8:00 p.m.

June 13   Arrived Haifa, Israel, on Sunday at 3:00 p.m.
and disembark at 10:30 p.m.

June 14   Arrived American Consulate, Tel Aviv, Israel,
about 1:00 a.m.

June 15   Departed Tel Aviv on Tuesday 7:20 a.m. for Paris
Arrived Paris at noon
Departed Paris at 1:15 p.m. for JFK, New York
Arrived JFK at 3:10 p.m.
Departed for Washington National Airport, DC,
at 4:05 p.m.
Arrived Washington National Airport at 5:15 p.m.
No bags!
Met by car and arrived home in Ashland, Virginia

Saturday, May 22, 1982

6:50 p.m. at the airport

After being in Beirut for a week in March, and then the wonderful spiritual experiences on the retreat in April, it is so hard for me to leave family and friends. During this time I have also begun to feel uncomfortable about going back to Beirut this one last time. I don't know why, though. It just does not feel right. So I thought it would be hard to say good-bye to everyone. But it was not. The sadness and lingering fear were already talked out with everyone. I do realize that I'll have to cope with those emotions in the next days, but for now I seem okay. It hurts inside though very badly, but I am at peace with myself if I let myself be.

I am going to try to write more legibly in this diary on this trip. I've not done so well in previous diaries. I've had lots of trouble re-reading the earlier ones when I tried to share them back home.

Missing my family and friends is going to be the really hard part of this trip. I really need them lately, since the Curcillo. I am so fragile regarding what I have learned about myself, of love and being loved. I don't want this thin shell of an ego to crack, or even worse, to break.

It is now 7:00 p.m. and we are on board the transit bus to the airplane. It is one of those buses that goes up and down, the whole thing, to move the people from the terminal to the level of the plane, and it can travel all over Dulles Airport.

7:25 p.m.

We are on board at last and I'm b.s.-ing with a lady from Bethesda, Maryland, who is going to London. She is really friendly and has offered me some candy. I enjoy talking to her; she is very down-to-earth and genuine. Her husband seems quite irritated that she is so friendly to those of us nearby on the plane.

Guess I'll settle in. I'll write later as I have time.

8:25 p.m.

I decided not to watch the movie "On Golden Pond" but to rest for those two hours.   They will be the only real rest I may get. I'm not much for movies anyway, so why bother.

10:00 p.m.

I just turned my watch ahead to 4:00 a.m. and I'm going to take a catnap. We just had dinner and it was very boring. There was a salad and roll, cheese and crackers, chicken, rice, peas and some chocolate cake.

I'm very tired and we land in three hours so I'll relax now. What else can I do?

Sunday, May 23, 1982

6:50 a.m.

We were awakened for a little continental breakfast at 5:30 a.m. I'm so tired that I ache. My eyes are bloodshot and burn; I just threw a little water on them but it did not help.

I slept for an hour after a bit of prayer to relax me. I prayed for my family especially, hoping that they may feel serenity now and throughout my absence. And I prayed for me and for all of us that we may grow and be happy. I'm going to miss them all so much.

7:40 a.m.

We arrived here in London at Heathrow Airport about a half hour ago and I've got nearly three hours before my next flight. I'd like to sleep, or at least rest, if I could. I'll read the letter I found in my carry-on from the family first; I was pleased with the little surprise letter that they gave me when I departed at the airport.

It was a nice letter. Thank you for it.

10:05 a.m.

I just got checked into my Mid-East flight to Beirut and it looks like a good number of people here. I am surprised to see so many people going to Beirut on a Sunday morning.

I sat at the airport for an hour, alone, with a pretext of sleep, but mostly watched people. There were lots of Indians, mostly women with children, it seemed. A fellow who sat down beside me struck up a conversation and we talked for the last one and one half hours. I bought him a cup of coffee too. His name is Bill Reese from Los Angeles. He is a marketing executive for dental supplies with a worldwide market firm and he has been in South Africa for six weeks. Before that he was home with his wife and kids for twenty days, and before that he was away in Australia, Japan and Singapore for three months! Can you imagine the travel and time away?

We've been in flight for about three hours now. I catnapped for a while, then we had beverages and nuts and lunched. The lunch was okay but I wasn't hungry. That was my fourth meal or snack since I left last night, and that has been only twelve hours, despite the apparent midday sun outside the plane. There were some things from the lunch tray that I decided to save for later this evening in Beirut: some cheese and crackers, and an apple. That way I won't have to exchange any money or go shopping tonight.

I'm not lonely or hurting inside today, like I was on my last trip to Beirut. My spiritual growth and my heightened belief in my family and their ability to believe in me are the main reasons, I think.

They've announced that we will arrive in about one hour.

I've heard from Khalil Bitar, M.D., who dropped off those letters at the house on Saturday, that there were three terrorist bombs set off in West Beirut last Friday. I heard about it in London too from some people on this flight. I do hope it is not a time of war or terrorism while I'm here. I would not want anyone back home to see the newspapers or hear the radio reports of such things. (But do not worry if you do, please.) Now I will rest again.

8:55 p.m. in Beirut

It's late and I'm ready for bed. I don't know quite how to tell what has happened to me since arriving here. But it is as extreme as it was on my last trip (or the time when I was in rural Egypt), except in the reverse direction! Instead of dreadful, it is wonderful. I'd better sit down to write all this.

I arrived on time in Beirut and learned that a fellow two seats away from me on the plane was also coming to teach for three weeks in the MPH program at AUB. His name is Colin Newell from London, a young doctoral student, I think. Anyway, we promised to meet later this week as we talked together on the ride to Beirut. They dropped him off at the Mayflower Hotel where I stayed when I was here two years ago. They brought me to Marquand House, the AUB presidential mansion. As it turns out, the new AUB president won't be here until July, so they are housing me and an Italian professor here.

I entered the place and felt overwhelmed at such a mansion. But I followed the house servant to the second floor to my bedroom, sitting/living room, and bath. I changed and went running right away; it was very invigorating to run my regular ten kilometers. I was suddenly very relaxed.

I ran with a fellow named Alex whom I had seen a dozen times (but had never met) when I was here in March.

Then I came back and showered and met the Italian professor

whose name I can't figure out. He is about 38 years old and quite delightful.

Now here's the scoop! He and I are the guests in the mansion with its staff of servants and we have access to any and all services - food, beverages, etc. We were served dinner formally with crystal and silver, all kinds of booze, wine, and a wonderful meal, with liquors ready in the living room afterwards. (Too bad I don't drink!) We are both kings, we have decided.

We learned that our rooms will be cleaned daily. There is a laundress who will do our clothes daily and have them back in two hours and a refrigerator near our bedrooms full of beverages too.

We get to choose the meal times and the people with whom we want to dine. I suppose we can select and/or approve menus too. Our butler is Hassan and the cook is Mohammed, and they have nothing to do except meet our needs, it seems.

"Are you sure you would not like some Cointreau or brandy with that coffee?" he just asked me again.

He just brought a bottle of ice water to my room for during the night. I'll bet he shines my shoes tomorrow and every other day!

Can you believe that I've been squirreling away crackers, napkins, peanut butter, cheese, etc. for my food? I had to do that on prior trips, but not this time. I've got a cook and a server, and can eat from crystal, silver and china in a formal dining room!

Dear Lord, I know I asked you to make me safe and happy here so that I could enjoy this time alone, but I didn't realize how great is your bounteous goodness! Thank you for making me feel so special.

We were even served packages of cigarettes with our drinks before and after dinner. [That I don't smoke seems odd to them since nearly everyone here smokes.]

Maybe I am dreaming. I'm not really in a hundred-year-old mansion, overlooking the Mediterranean Sea. The Italian professor (I just have to figure out his name.) and I have decided we will take turns being president of AUB. Tomorrow is my turn.

Monday, May 24, 1982

7:25 a.m.

I went to bed at about ten last night and slept until nearly six a.m., but stayed in bed until just before seven. I'm still very tired and would like to go back to bed. I couldn't sleep, but I sure could rest. Maybe I'll have the chance to do so later on, but somehow I doubt it very much.

I have a sore throat this morning. I noticed it starting on the plane when I inhaled so much smoke from one of the other passenger's many cigarettes. I surely do not need a cold.

8:25 a.m.

I am finishing up a breakfast of bacon and eggs, toast and oranges. There was a big explosion about twenty minutes ago, followed by gunfire nearby. The radio said there was an explosion by the French Embassy and it caused a fire. I hope no one was killed.

I know there were deaths though. One can feel it when a bomb like that goes off. No one will say anything to me, I am sure.

The Italian professor and I just kept on eating during the explosion. We asked ourselves if we should stop, or be upset, or something. We were both embarrassed to be so blasé; we felt we should feel or do something.

So now I know what a bomb sounds like.

10:10 a.m.

I heard that at least ten people were killed in the explosion and about the same number were injured.

I met my chairman Nabil and have worked on my classes. I teach from 10:30 a.m. to 12:30 p.m. on Monday, Wednesday and Friday; on Tuesday and Thursday, it is 8:00 a.m. to 10:00 a.m. So I'll be off to class shortly now.

I went to the bank and got some cash too. I exchanged $35 U.S. and the rate was 4.95 Lebanese lira which is quite high; even higher than last time. I don't need much, but I will in time.

I also wrote a letter home which I mailed today. Hope the mail works; if not, they'll be reading this diary soon enough anyway.

Letter home
Monday morning, May 24, 1982

Dear all,

I arrived here safely after an uneventful trip. It is nice weather here, like at home. I start my work today and my teaching too, but am very tired. However, I slept last night here, although not the night on the plane.

I left you at 7:00 and got on the plane where we ate dinner at 9:00 p.m. as we flew toward London. By midnight the sun was up and it was nearly breakfast time. It was a very short night.

I am not staying at the same apartment as last time. Indeed, I'm a guest at the AUB presidential home. It is a huge and wonderful mansion, about one hundred years old. There is no president until July and so two of us visiting professors are guests here. I have a bedroom and sitting room and bath, and full use of the house <u>and its staff</u>. All my meals are cooked and served to me, my laundry is done for me, even my room is cleaned. When I sit downstairs, I am offered coffee, beverages and cigarettes by the staff. What a treat to be made to feel like a king.

The other visiting professor is from Bologna, Italy, a computer engineer and very delightful. We are both enjoying this house and are overwhelmed by it.

It is too early to tell how my trip will go, but I have a positive attitude. I am not depressed or scared or lonely. I have my Good News and other books, my running, and my work. So I suppose I'll be just fine, if I don't get overworked. If I have my way, it won't happen.

I thought of you at the closing of the CCD program and at the Crone's party. I am sorry to miss them, but I cannot do everything, I know. There will be other occasions.

I hope all the girls are well. Sara and Elizabeth, be sure to help Mom and your little sisters while I am away. Rebecca and Tressa, play nicely and share your things.

I'll be home soon.

I love you all.   *Chuck, Daddy*

2:10 p.m.

I taught my class and let them out at noon. There are ten students and it went pretty well, I thought. Then I saw Nadim Karam, M.D., my dear friend from my visit here last March. I gave him all the packages I had for him from the U.S. Then I invited him to lunch at Marquand House with me.

We had a nice talk and were joined by the Italian professor (whose name I have learned is Luigi Cerofolini) and one of his colleagues. We had a delightful lunch discussing Lebanon. The food was good and so attractively presented too. As a result, I ate too much.

I also learned that Colin Newell has been moved from the Mayflower Hotel to here at Marquand House. Now there will be three of us here to take turns being the president of AUB. I am very pleased because I found Colin quite friendly.

I have been asked to go to a lecture of Nadim's. So I'm off for now.

The green field at the American University of Beirut.

6:00 p.m.

I just got back from running down on the "green field,"
the soccer field along the corniche of the sea wall. It is right
in front of Marquand House, about a third of a mile. Now I
think I will sit awhile and maybe write some letters. I've got
to prepare my two-hour lecture for 8:00 a.m. tomorrow too.
But I think I'll work on that later tonight after dinner. I'm
having a problem deciding what and how to teach here this
time. I can't understand what I'd been planning when I wrote
the course outline a couple of months ago. I need to rethink
the whole course or at least the first part so it meets the needs
of the students I have. [They are mostly all physicians, toward
the end of their training, I think.]

Running my 6.2 miles down on the green field was quite delightful again today. The sea breezes, the smells of tropical plants and flowers, and the sights of the city and the sea all blend into a magic that is hypnotizing.

I enjoyed Nadim's class today too. It seems that he has some very good students, but I don't think mine seem to be so good.

9:00 p.m.

I sat outside on the grounds under the trees of Marquand House and read a bit of Thomas Merton before dinner. There are gardenias in bloom nearby which is about the only thing I know of that could smell better than the sea/flora aroma of the green field. Colin and I dined together on spaghetti and meat sauce and a wonderful salad. Fresh fruit and cookies came next. We went for a walk in the dark afterward and I enjoyed his company very much. He is a demographer, aged 27, single and in love with a girl in London.

We are back at the House now and are having a drink together; his is arak, the traditional Lebanese drink and mine is ginger ale. The house staff cannot figure out why I do not drink all their fancy liquors.

I guess. Who knows?

Tuesday, May 25, 1982

6:30 a.m.

Up and at 'em. I got up at 5:45 and prayed and read and am now ready for travel to Baalbek. It should be a real adventure, and maybe we'll get to see the archeological ruins too, not just the UNICEF project.

A wonderful breakfast again: a grapefruit half, sweeter than any I have ever had, and two croissants, one filled with zatar (a mixture of herbs dominated by oregano) and the other with cheese. The usual bowl of gardenia flowers afloat on water is sitting on the table and it makes a strong fragrance in the room. Mohammed picks them fresh every morning, I think.

Did I tell you about the wailing woman outside of my classroom building yesterday? She had just heard of the death of one of the people in the morning bombing at the French Embassy, and she became hysterical and started to scream and wail. It lasted for about two minutes. The students in my class became agitated and upset, wouldn't sit down, and stayed at the windows. Later they said that it was a traditional and socially-defined way to behave, that is, to mourn publicly and loudly. But it was very upsetting because they too knew the man for whom the mourner was crying. He was a male nurse from the AUB Hospital.

5:05 p.m.

I returned from my visit to the Bekaa Valley and Baalbek a few minutes ago. I saw the Roman ruins of the city of Heliopolis from the car. Lots of columns and a major part of the cathedral are the main parts remaining. We went to the AUB agricultural farms and interviewed the director about the area. Then we went to the municipal health office in Baalbek, and then to the regional hospital there. The regional hospital has nearly 100 beds, and no nurses, except for five rather poorly trained nuns who volunteer there. It was a nice place, but in pathetic shape due to no staff, no money, and politics.

On the way back we stopped at Zahle for lunch. We had Lebanese food and relaxed along the river at the café. This town was the site of last year's "Zahle missile crisis."

We also learned that there was a fight in the skies over Beirut today and a Syrian plane was shot down by an Israeli plane. This will probably mean more violence. I only hope that it is not in the American newspapers. It's okay here, but it would sound bad to read about it, I think.

Today I was tired and remain so. The jet lag and loss of sleep are catching up with me. Also, my companions chose to speak Arabic most of the time and I became quite bored. The combination of jet lag and all-Arabic has done me in for today.

When I came into my room just now, all my laundry was done and neatly pressed, even my running clothes!

I had cod, peas and French fries for dinner. Colin dined with me. Then we had our coffee in the living room. It is always served there and there are liquors afterward. Later I wrote a letter to Ted M and one to Ann S. I am told that the post is working okay so I am going to find out. I will try to read awhile now and then go to bed. My letter-writing was interrupted by a lot of shooting down on the corniche by the green field. There must be some crazies out this evening. It scared Colin and me for a moment as it seemed as if it were on campus. God forbid that they ever get into the compound of AUB!

I'm lonesome for my family tonight. While writing to Ted, I was lonesome to see him too. I thought of everyone I love and wished I were with them. Just a word or a touch and I could come back here revitalized for another while. When the loneliness gets bad (as it will), should I fight it and go on, or give in to it and hurt, and maybe get useless? I had not thought about it before. What do I do?

REPORT ON FIELD TRIP TO
QAZA OF BAALBECK
May 25, 1982

INTRODUCTION:

This field trip was organized in response to the interest of UNICEF and the HSA Department in the Organization of programs directed towards improvement of the health status of the area.

The group that participated in this field trip was

Miss Leila Sasr - UNICEF

Dr. Nabil Kronfol

Dr. C. Breindel

Dr. N. Karam

Activities:

I. *The 1st meeting was with Dr. Fawwak Sleiman, Director of the A.U.B. Farm. Several issues were addressed during this meeting and the following points were specifically noted.*

1. *Estimated population of the Triangle including Tannin, Baalbeck of Deir al Ahmar is 250,000.*
Estimated population of Baalbeck area is 150,000.

2. *Any program should have specific objectives specially so since the area is in great need for programs addressing various aspects of health care.*

3. *The value of upgrading and coordinating with existing non-profit organizations was stressed.*

4. *Means of interaction with practicing physicians should be given special attention.*

5. *The Municipalities are very weak and their contribution towards health care is minimal.*

6. *Very small % of the population benefit from N.S.S.F.*

7. *Water and sewage treatment does not exist.*

8. *Dirty water supply from YAMMOUNEH Lake.*

9. *Inadequate facilities for care of agricultural accidents.*
10. *The A.U.B. Farm may have a role within this program.*

II. *The second activity was a visit to the Governmental Dispensary at Baalbeck in an attempt to meet with Dr. Kanawati. Unfortunately Dr. Kanawati was not available and some information was obtained from the clerk.*

1. *Since the onset of civil conflict in Lebanon the dispensary stopped providing any curative services.*

2. *The dispensary still offers vaccinations and a "lot" of people come for that.*

3. *There are about 25 employees that serve within this dispensary in the implementation of several programs. However, it was felt that some of these programs are not currently operating.*

4. *The different political parties are currently dominating the health care delivery system.*

5. *The vaccines that were present at the dispensary's refrigerator were all out dated.*

III. *The third activity was a visit to the Government Hospital at Baalbeck where the group met with Dr. Omeiri who is the Chief of Staff and Director of the Hospital. Discussion centered on issues related to problems that the hospital faces and to potential solutions on these problems. Issues noted were:*

1. *Limited funds*

2. *Red tape in dealing with the Ministry of Health*

3. *Poor salary scales*

4. *Dominance of the private sector and political parties*

5. *Lack of qualified personnel, etc.*

DISCUSSION:

It was evident, from the visit, that there are great potentials for program support and development in the field of Health Care in this area of Lebanon. Support of the existing services and on facilities seems to be a better alternative than the creation of new ones. It was also noted that the development of a comprehensive program that addresses most if not all of the needs, is very difficult and very expensive and that small programs with specific and limited objectives may be a better alternative.

Issues that these programs may address include:
a. Upgrading of some of the departments and/or services within the government hospital.
b. Support of the local non profit health care delivery units
c. Addressing certain aspects of environmental health and sewage disposal
d. Improving the quality of supplies within the governmental dispensary
e. Initiation of Health Education Programs and upgrading of school health programs
f. Initiation of continuing education programs for Health Professionals in the area
g. Using the government Hospital as a site for the training of para-medical staff.

Submitted by
Nadim Karan

Some students accompany Dr. Breindel for an outing.

Wednesday, May 26, 1982

8:30 a.m.

I got up at 6:15 a.m. and had breakfast with Colin, then I got my class notes together. It is a beautiful day, after a rainstorm during the night. The aroma of the sea air! I am now at work and about ready for my course this morning. I surely have a low interest in the course and my class at this point. The trip yesterday, second day of class, stole my thunder, I think. However, I am going to try and reorganize this first week of lectures, choose some decent readings and get rid of the book chosen for the students by the Department. For now I'll relax and get organized.

My goal today is to get some organization into my work

here. I need to make a list of people to contact and things to do and then go do it. Amen!

9:20 a.m.

I just went uptown to deliver the package that Kahlil Bitar brought me last Saturday. I had trouble finding the place, but I met Mohammed, our cook, who showed me how to find it. Mr. Bitar was a shy man, so I was polite and as brief as I could be. He will probably call and invite me to lunch later on during my stay, now that he knows I have arrived here. I look forward to that.

I stopped and got a manooshe (a warm flatbread with olive oil and zatar on it, served from kiosks along the street) on the way back here. Boy, those things are good. I love that kind of food for breakfast too. Also I've convinced our cook to prepare Lebanese food for dinner tonight, so I hope it is good too.

12:50 p.m.

I taught my class for two rather boring hours. The students are rather lazy, uninterested and uninspiring. It is not like before. I have identified only two exceptions so far. The class is mostly women who have little chance for a job and who have given up on school, it seems. They came to school to find a husband and/or because they did not get jobs. They admit that. They chose their majors in health services administration naively, but they now realize that there are no jobs to be had for a Master of Public Health (MPH) in Administration in Lebanon. But in three weeks they graduate and they don't much care about their two block courses between now and then. In summary, it is a quite dismal group for me. What I teach them, they will never be able to use and they know it.

I see that the bombing of the French Embassy is on the

first page of the *Herald Tribune* so I expect they have heard all about it in the U.S. too. I guess there is nothing much to say; I hope they don't overreact and worry about me. Considering that I'm sitting in the sun on the patio of a mansion overlooking the sea and surrounded by flowers and tropical gardens, it does not seem that they need to worry.

I left a note for Nabil to inquire about the status of our research project and proposed book today. We have not discussed it and I suspect that either it did not get approved or else his interest is waning since my March visit. It is okay with me, because I have plenty else to do. I won't complain if my Lebanese connection is severed after this visit. However, I have invested a lot of my life in this book and research in Lebanon.

6:40 p.m.

A nice afternoon of work after I lunched alone. Mohammed made Lebanese sandwiches and lentil soup and homemade cookies.

I wrote up my lecture for tomorrow then met with Nabil. He gave me lots of materials to read on Lebanon but told me we haven't gotten our funding for the research to do the book yet. However, the book can still be done, even without funding, he thinks.

I've lost interest in it though. Now that I know there are not funds for a return trip, I can say adieu to the research and the book. I'll feign some interest, as I can, but mostly I'll enjoy myself and meet people on this trip.

A student wants me to go to Sidon for the day and see the Hariri Medical Center where my friend Bassam Kawwass once worked. I hoped to go there too, perhaps next week. Also, I am going to go to Brummana in the mountains with Nadim Karam on Sunday morning until Monday morning.

He and his wife are opening a family practice center in this village in the mountains. They are both family practitioners. It should be very nice. I am also invited out with the Dean and Nabil and their wives for dinner on Friday. So I have lots going on.

Letter home
May 26, 1982 9:25 p.m. Wednesday

Dear dears,

I'm about ready for bed now, but can't seem to get in the mood for sleep. I read my Order of Reunion card earlier and wrote out some brief answers. I'll send it to one of the guys when I write them. It is a dull and short exercise alone.

I am well, but having a few "lonely" pangs. It is lovely here and I enjoy my two house mates very much. (Did I tell you? On Monday the delightful English fellow I met on the plane moved out of his hotel to here. He's Colin Newell, a demographer from London, age 27, and funny.) I like staying here too. The service is grand, especially the daily laundry. My clothes are done every morning and returned folded like new. The food is good but very American; we've asked for more Lebanese food, and started to get it today. Little old Mohammed is quite the cook and baker - he even makes the jams, marmalades and ketchup.

I teach two hours per day and it is really dull. Most of the students are young females who came here to get husbands and/or jobs, and with graduation only three weeks away, they have neither and are sad. It is a hard group to motivate.

Yesterday I didn't teach but went with Nabil, Nadim and two people from UNICEF up over the mountain and into the fertile Bekaa Valley of Lebanon. We were looking at a possible UNICEF health program and we interviewed several people there. It was nice to escape much of the war-torn area of old Beirut. We lunched about 2:00 p.m. on the way back in Zahle, the capital of the Bekaa. It was the site of last year's Zahle missile crisis which canceled my trip here.

I learned from Nabil that our research and book have not been funded. We could do it anyway, and he is pushing me to work in it. But I just smile. I'll not be back here again without that funding, it seems, so I'll just teach and enjoy myself.

I'm invited (or will be soon, actually) to Sidon to see Hariri Medical Center where Bassam was employed. I hope to go there for an afternoon next week. One of my students is doing a project there on planning and has made the trip possible.

Also my dear friend and office colleague Nadim Karam, M.D., the doctor (with the three kids born on the same day March 1, 1981 and again 1982) has invited me to come to his mountain village on Sunday and return on Monday. It is quite rural and traditional, he tells me, and I'll sleep on the floor. I am eager to go.

Nabil has accepted to be the Dean of Makassud Medical School across town as of July 1, but will keep his role here. He would like to step down as chair, I think. And I know whom he would like to become his successor.

Please keep notes for me so you can tell me about the things happening there. Pray for me and us as I do, and relax. There is going to be a period of political "crisis" soon here, and its major effect will be a media blitz in the western newspapers, we are being told. Ignore it all, as it is an attempt to show problems so that some foreign interests will get involved here.

I am well; I love you all.

Chuck and Daddy

10:00 p.m.

Dinner was nice and all three of us were there. We had pita and baba-ghannouge (smashed and pureed eggplant), a dish of rice and a plate of lamb, with Roman beans in a sauce. There was a plate of akedinia (a fruit, maybe a loquat) and oranges and freshly baked cookies too.

Later I wrote a letter home. I was nervous then because I heard shooting at least four times in the background while I was writing.

I like the way we dine here. It is teaching me to relax and to eat slower. I also like the idea of sitting together and talking after dinner away from the table. I wonder if we could rethink how we eat and dine as a family. I would like it a lot and so would you all, I'll bet. Ask me about it when you read this.

Thursday, May 27, 1982

6:50 a.m.

I'm up and ready for some breakfast. I was noticing how high in the sky the sun is. I'll bet they don't have daylight-saving time here in Lebanon. I wonder if that makes our change in time six or seven hours from Virginia. I never was good at figuring that sort of thing out.

I'm full of bug bites. The mosquitos must be terrible here as I heard Colin and Luigi complaining too.

10:55 a.m.

My class went okay and I've been invited out by two of my students. One of them (Samira) invited me to go to Biblos on the coastal area north of here on Saturday, and another Raymond, pronounced the French way, invited me to his home for the evening and overnight next week. I will continue to accept all such invitations as I can.

I went to run before lunch as it was so nice and I was in the mood. Also the house will have guests attending meetings all afternoon and I don't want to go by them during the late afternoon in my running shorts, and all sweaty. It was hot in the sun but I felt good as there were few people on the green field running and I could relax. In the late afternoon, it is always very crowded.

Luigi joined Colin and me for lunch today. He was scared.

He had been on Bliss Street. It runs along the south side of the AUB compound wall. He saw shots being fired only five meters away. There were shots in the air, probably in order to be frightening. But the police came and fired back. Meanwhile, Luigi hid behind a car and then ran to the AUB gate. It was nothing but a typical incident here, but it was comic to hear Luigi's story. When so many people have guns, it is common for them to shoot into the air to get attention or, in this case, to break up a crowded street.

4:45 p.m.

I just realized something. I have nothing to do! No housework, no laundry, no schoolwork, just nothing!

I left the office after about three o'clock because my work was done and I was bored. I walked about town, bought a half-dozen cookies and a chocolate pastry, then came home and had a feast. Now I found some books and chose Paul Gallico's short story *The Snow Goose* to read. It was quite sad and beautiful at the same time, and I was moved by it. Now I have two hours until dinner for relaxing here on the veranda.

9:05 p.m.

I went for a walk after dinner and prayed. Then I came back here to Marquand House and read a bit. I'm particularly rested after a good and calm day. We had another Lebanese dinner too - grape leaves and rice-stuffed kousa, those little squashes, and pita. There were fresh strawberries for dessert too. We overate tremendously, both Colin and I. We seem to be good at that. However, we have both noticed that the service has gotten simpler and less frequent. We think that we are casual and not demanding at all, so the staff is rising only to the level of our expectations. And that is just fine with us.

I walked in town a while again this afternoon and saw several places where the streets were recently repaired with blacktop and that surprised me. It will be amazing to consider by whom and how such repairs were made.

Friday, May 28, 1982

8:35 a.m.

I was hoping to sleep in today, but awakened at 6:40 and lay there until seven. I talked to myself and daydreamed as I usually do first thing in the morning. Then I got washed and dressed.

One of my students who was trying to arrange for me to visit Hariri Medical Center just came by. He told me that he received a call from there saying that I could not come as they had changed their minds. The student told me (with much embarrassment) that the place is poorly managed and that they don't want me to see what they are doing, and not doing. What a pain in the butt they are to be that way! As if I'd ever be critical or nosey! However, the student says that he will take me to Sidon for a visit anyway, just to look around and see the sights. Perhaps I could even call upon Bassam's parents who are there.

1:00 p.m.

It is lunch time and I am at home. I am feeling very bored and lonely today. I seem to have no particular ambition to do anything either. I guess I am disappointed in things this trip. This morning I prepared my class, then walked to town and saw Elias Nsar at his jewelry store. That is where I bought things on earlier trips. I told him I would come by on Tuesday to look at a couple of gold chain bracelets for my family members. (You have to give them advance notice before they will get out any of the gold items, I have learned. Due to safety and security, they keep very little there at the shop and only bring in a full selection if they have a client.)

I only taught for an hour due to my nose and sinuses, which are in bad shape today. These wonderful aromas of the sea and the fauna are a bit deceiving for me. I can get some antihistamines without a prescription here, but I'll get medical advice from Nadim or Nabil. Nadim did not come in today, nor did he call. I suppose that he will try to call me sometime to let me know when and where he will meet me this weekend to visit him.

4:40 p.m.

A slow afternoon again. I lunched first with Colin at the House on soup, sandwiches and fruit. The cherries are so nice just now. Then Colin left, and Luigi came and I kept him company at his lunch. He leaves tomorrow to go to Bologna and is glad to go, but is also quite satisfied with his nine days here.

Then I went to the office and wrote my exam for my students. A student Haytham Hajjar came by to discuss his paper on commissioning a hospital. Then he sent me off to both libraries in a frustrated look for references for him. I also learned that my packet of readings for the class has disappeared from the reserved section of the library. The students, it seems, are in a dither about preparing for the classes and the examination without the readings.

I saw Nadim too. He will pick me up on Sunday at ten o'clock in the morning to go to his home in Brummana overnight. He says there is a Lebanese wedding on Sunday afternoon and he will try to get me invited to come along with him and his wife. I'd like that very much, of course. He's Orthodox and I guess the wedding will be in an Orthodox church.

Tomorrow at ten I'm going to the ancient city and ruins of Jbiel (called Biblos, in ancient times) with Samira and Hala, two of my students. It is considered the oldest city in the world and has one temple dating from at least the 32nd century B.C. Imagine that! 3,400 years ago! There are Phoenician, Greek, Roman, Turkish, and Crusader antiquities and ruins there. I look forward to the visit immensely and am confident that it is a safe area to visit.

I'm going to Nabil and Lina's tonight. I assume it will be a home dinner and that Dean Haroute Armenian and his wife Soma will come too. I have to get dressed shortly for that fete.

I have become so casual every evening here. I came in from running about six or later and asked for a tray of tea, and just sat there on the veranda until dinner. Tonight I got a plate of goat cheese and pita too, because dinner will be so late, probably about ten p.m., as is the Lebanese custom (ala France).

I am feeling better tonight after my day of melancholy.

11:50 p.m.

I went to Nabil's place for a drink, then to a French restaurant with them. It was nice and relaxing. I was back by eleven. Luigi arrived shortly after I did, and Colin was still up. So we raided the refrigerator for beer and b.s.-ed for a while. Tomorrow Luigi leaves so we had a nice talk. He is a nice man. We'll miss him.

Saturday, May 29, 1982

8:35 a.m.

I didn't sleep well last night due to the mosquitoes and general restlessness. I finally awoke at 5:30 but lay there for an hour. Then I got up and read while sitting on the patio among the flowers and shrubs. It was a peaceful way to sit while watching the sea down below.

We all breakfasted together and it was Luigi's last time with us. We joked and exchanged addresses, as if to suggest that our friendship would be renewed in the future when we should be able to visit each other. It is amazing how we have grown together in such a short time - sort of colleagues in arms in Marquand House.

Luigi has offered to post a letter home for me from Italy this weekend. So I'll quickly write before I go to meet my ride to Jbiel.

Letter home, May 29, 1982, Saturday morning, 8:45 a.m.

Dear all,

Luigi is returning to Bologna, Italy today and has offered to post a letter for us as it will save nearly a week in transit to the USA. So I'll quick dash off a note to you before I must go to meet my ten o'clock ride. It is difficult to decide what to tell you as I write you several times a day in my little diary. So I am not sure what I have told you yet.

Yesterday I was sad and melancholy, due to loneliness. But I am better today. I've been teaching two hours and it is dull and the students are not interested. It is a real drudge. I've done little else, as I've decided to relax. There is no point in the work plan we had planned with Nabil unless I know there a possibility to come back and continue it. Since I don't expect to be able to return, I'm just relaxing and enjoying Lebanon and myself.

I am really eating a lot here but have not had any terrific food yet. I'm just enjoying being served so much. However, I expect to really do some good eating this weekend. I'm going north along the coast to Jbiel (or originally Biblos) this morning. It is the oldest town in the world, once the center of papyrus-making in the pre-Egyptian era. Its name signifies the paper on which the evangelists wrote the Good News, and so the word "bible" comes from the ancient name of the town. Two of my students will take me there, and we will return by late afternoon.

Tomorrow after Mass, Nadim Karam has invited me to the mountain suburb of Beirut, called Brummana, where he lives. I'll return on Monday morning then. He has a relative who will be married on Sunday afternoon and hopes to take me to the wedding too, so that should be fun, if we go.

I am well and very relaxed. I still plan to return home on Saturday evening, June 12. There may be a way to get a same-day connection and not have to lay over in London (or somewhere else) on the way back. But plan on me then.

Today is the Moriarty's party there. Have a great time.

Nabil goes to Abu Dhabi all next week, so I'm at peace without any expectations for being dragged into any of his projects. That is both good and bad, I guess. I will be a bit bored perhaps, but I will also be free to do whatever I like. I have been invited to stay overnight (for dinner, but then stay until morning - nobody here travels at night) at a student's home on Wednesday. He and his wife have a baby and the student's father is a former Minister of Health here. I will plan to go. I also have been invited to spend an afternoon visiting Sidon and I am excited to go. Perhaps I will be able to call on Bassam's parents there. I don't know how though.

I hope you are all well. I think of you constantly and pray for you daily. I love you all dearly. These times away from you teach me to appreciate and understand the importance of our lives and love.

All my love.   Chuck and Daddy

4:40 p.m.

I returned from Jbiel about a half hour ago and discovered that I had been moved from my rooms to the room that had been occupied by Luigi. It seems that the painters want to do my rooms next, so I have been moved. I do resent someone else moving all my things about, however. Of course, I had to go and find the one-third of my things that were not moved. I like this room better, even though it does not have a separate living room or a desk. It has a nice bath and a pretty view out over the patio and out toward the harbor.

My trip to Jbiel was great! I had walked uptown to exchange a twenty-dollar bill and got the same rate as last Monday. Because I planned to be away today and tomorrow, I thought I had better have some more money with me.

Hala could not join us, but Samira and I went across Beirut to the East side and up the coast through Junieh and then on to Jbiel. Jbiel is overshadowed by the antiquity. It is like Williamsburg is to us, I think, a place of restored history and pride and tradition. The enormous French Crusaders' castle dominates everything else there. It has a walled city with an enormous and tall castle nearly nine hundred years old. We toured all through it by ourselves and got lost in the dark and dingy labyrinth of stairs and halls. It sits quite unattended by guides or controls. It is partly fallen in, but quite impressive. In its environs are the detailed remains of a medieval city, a Roman city with temples, and an amphitheater and, would you believe, a 3,400-year-old Phoenician city and harbor! There is the rubble of one age built on another, and it is confusing to see it all on the precipice of the sea.

The sea there is clear and beautiful, and it is a popular resort area. We watched bathers and boaters and then ate in a café overlooking a small port of Jbiel. Several pleasure boats full of "beautiful people" and jet-setters came in and ate the excellent Lebanese cuisine too.

We had a bowl of vegetables (served whole, with sharp knives) and hummus, baba-hanooj, and pita, then a couple of shish tawook, the roasted chicken on a skewer which I just love.

This new area of Lebanon, the eastern or Christian area, is another world. It is much cleaner than western Beirut and, after leaving Beirut city, there are no ravages of war to be seen. In Jbiel, we could not tell there had ever been a terrible war here in 1976.

We rode along a coastal highway and the high and steep mountain peaks were just a half mile in from the shore and highway, it seemed. There were churches and cathedrals and monasteries overhanging the highest cliffs. At one place there is a ski lift from the sea to the top of the mountains - nearly a mile long and as high. We were going to ride one of the cars on the way back but did not have time to do so. Samira has suggested that we will go there next Saturday if I were interested and we could get a party together. Then we could lunch in the mountains. It sounds nice, and I'll hope to do it. But I'll wait a bit and check on my options first.

I was going to run when I got back, but will wait until later as there is a soccer game down on the green field and I can't run until it is done.

The mountains along the coast north of Beirut

10:00 p.m.

I am ready for bed and hope to sleep well as I have a busy day tomorrow, beginning with Mass at 7:30 a.m. Then I'm off to Brummana with Nadim.

Colin bought a half kilo of mixed nuts, the kind that are served in Lebanese homes just before dinner. We ate quite a few and now it is hard to lie down and rest. We had a casual Saturday night supper, with meat patties, fries and sliced raw vegetables, and then fruit for dessert. Good night.

Sunday, May 30, 1982

6:45 a.m.

I am in a quandary because I have been up since six and cannot seem to find Mohammed to make my breakfast. And I don't know my way around the kitchen here. I did manage a half of a grapefruit for my breakfast and have started on that.

Earlier I heard two big booms up in town. I cannot tell for sure, but I suspect that they were bombs. I do hope not. However, they were so distant that I don't think they could have been anything else.

I slept well in my new room but awakened early as usual. I suppose it is the early sunrise that makes me wake up early; since they don't have daylight-saving time, I must be up by 4:00 a.m. I do know that the sun goes down too early, by seven thirty in the evening.

10:35 p.m. in Brummana

I'm just into bed after a long day here in Brummana with Nadim and Huda Karam. He picked me up at eleven, after I'd gone to a Mass in French and then run laps on the green field. We have had a nice day and I will write about it tomorrow. For now I am dead tired. It is good to be tired today because I worked, helping to fix up the Karam's clinic, which opens this week. I also played with their babies - three of them: twins born March 1,1981, and a boy born March 1, 1982.

Both Nadim and Huda are physicians and have their M.P.H. too. They are quite nice and hard-working. I admire their guts to come back here from the United States after their residencies and to live so frugally. Their lives are simple; their apartment is meager. But they are rich inside. Good night.

Monday, May 31, 1982, back in Beirut

8:00 a.m.

We got up at 5:30, but I was awake for an hour before that, listening to the thunder. It started to rain and hail about 5:45 and it was a terrible and noisy storm. Nadim says it is the first time he can remember a rain at this time of year. It caused major traffic jams on the steep and winding roads so that it took us two hours to get back to Beirut. To top it all off, when we got there, the Syrian checkpoints were stopping every car. So there were literally thousands of cars backed up at the checkpoint. I just got to Marquand House now. I'll have some breakfast quickly, shower, and go to class. I am exhausted from the stressful trip, but not as badly as Nadim is.

Later after breakfast

The rain has stopped. I hope my shoes dry out quickly so that I can wear them today. I don't have another choice except for my black oxfords.

There was fighting in Beirut yesterday, in the south part of Beirut, between the Syrians and the Palestinians, I think. I also had heard that there were some bombs found in cars yesterday, but they were discovered before they could explode. The cook Mohammed says that there was quite a bit of fighting and he heard it. This is part of an increasing political unrest here due to three things. First, there was a speech in Chicago by General Alexander Haig, our Secretary of State, who spoke about Lebanon. This has caused tension and has angered some political sects. Second is the visit by Philip Habib next week; whenever he comes, all of the political groups fight in order to show a position of power and military strength before and during his visit. Third, the upcoming selection of a new president by Parliament is causing a juggling of power. All in all, it spells political tension and creates a time to show military might.

Yesterday morning I heard several booms in the early hours and thought it was bombing. What it was though was Israeli jets creating sonic booms over Beirut. They do that at least weekly, I was told. When I heard the thunder early this morning that is what I thought it was. Then when the thunder continued, I knew it had to be either war or thunder.

Let me write next about yesterday and my trip to the hillside town of Brummana. It is larger than I had thought, a nice size of a city on top of a mountain, from which the sea is visible and beautiful to see. It took about forty minutes with no traffic to wind back and forth up the mountain to Brummana. Nadim has a basement apartment in his family house which he and Huda are fixing up to be their family medicine clinic. They are living there too, very austerely and simply, with little furniture. They have made a medical office with three modern examination rooms, and it will open today. Huda will work the mornings and Nadim will work from 3:30 p.m. to 6:30 p.m. each day. It will be a long time before they pay off their investment and make any money. Meanwhile Nadim continues here at AUB and makes plans for them to move into a real apartment later this year. They are both very overworked and exhausted just now, and with three babies too! We had a nice traditional dinner on their porch yesterday, then drove around Brummana.

At 4:00 we came down to East Beirut for a wedding at an Eastern rite Catholic church. It was overflowing and we had to stand outside on the steps. What little I saw was super-ceremonial and tacky beyond my descriptive abilities. Would you believe it? There was a movie camera with lighting on booms over the crowd. Cameramen were roaming about capturing the service, the crowd, and every angle of the bride and groom. It was totally disruptive to the service and to anyone's ability to appreciate the purpose of the assemblage. Nadim said that it was a show of wealth by the bride's family as are many of the other things at a wedding here. Actually, when Nadim said we would go to a wedding earlier, I had expected a local wedding in the mountains with lots of quaint charm. Boy, was I ever wrong!

We returned to Brummana and I played with the baby Samir. Then we decided to work on the clinic, as there was still so much to be done. I helped put together shelves and stocked cabinets to help Huda, while Nadim got called out for two home visits. Next I painted a bench until Nadim returned. Then we went out to eat some pizza.

This village is a mountain resort community and, since the war, has really grown and prospered. People want to go to the mountains to escape and so Brummana thrives. There are many restaurants there and we ate in a cute little one. It was ten when we got there, and we were too tired to enjoy ourselves much. Normally, Nadim and Huda go to bed at 8:30 or 9:00 p.m., they said. They must get up at five each morning in order to get down to Beirut before the worst of the traffic.

Nadim teased me a lot about my going to church yesterday. People here do not go anymore, especially since the war, so I am weird to go, he says. There seems to be at least two types of people, we observed. There are those whose needs or concerns are basic material needs, like food and safety, and they just don't get to a level of concern about God or the meaning of life and self. For them, religion doesn't exist. Then there are others who once had religious beliefs but cannot now accept that God exists or that, if He exists, that He is good or just, since the war. They hate religion and God because God has not served their material and physical needs. So they reject religion and God as meaningless and, if their measure is their own physical sufficiency only, they are right.

I must go shower and get ready to go now.

12:45 p.m., back at home

I got paid this morning for my work. It is like a stipend. I was paid in cash, of course, all in U.S. one-hundred dollar bills. It is remarkable that they do this. I don't feel safe with it on my person.

My lecture went well, although I have decided to lecture only for one hour. Two hours is too long for such materials as these.

One of the students who works here in this department started off my class by asking me a question from last week's lectures. Her question was worded exactly as it is stated on my examination tomorrow. Given that I have been told (by the students) that cheating is not uncommon here, I suspect that she has a copy of my examination. The secretary, a lovely older lady, typed it and made copies last Friday. I wonder if she left the ditto master or some copies of the exam in the waste paper basket near the ditto machine. My suspicion is not just slight either, and I don't know what to do about something like this. I've never had something like this happen in the United States, but it may be more acceptable here, although not right. What do I do? What will I do if she distributed it around, or even to her other friends in the classroom? Ugh!

I'm trying to arrange a trip to Sidon for Friday. I'd like to call on Balsam's parents for a brief visit, if possible. I will ask another professor Eva if it is possible. She knows them and will know how to contact them too.

3:15 p.m.

After lunch I walked to town to get some Lebanese pastries

and Colin came with me, but was in a hurry. So, after a few minutes of a quick walk, we headed back to campus empty-handed. When I got to the office without my keys, I found myself locked out. So I went to the library. There I looked for materials on London in order to program my short stay there on my return trip back home. I found little of use except a few maps. Looking through the card catalog, I was struck to read the dates on the many books. Mostly they are from the 1960s or older. I found many books from the twenties, thirties and forties, and even some from the last century. Their library is greatly limited, due to its being overseas and rather dependent on philanthropy. I could find few books less than twelve years old. What a difficult thing, considering what is available to other comparable university students in the United States. We do not realize how fortunate we are, but take our abundance for granted.

9:20 p.m.

I ran early, about four, then showered and finished reading the Epistles in the New Testament I had brought along. (I got it on the Curcillo weekend.) Colin and I had a nice spaghetti dinner together, then I went for a walk alone. I wrote a couple of letters and now I'm in bed. I'm quite tired.

I am tired of being so intent on all of the noises in the environment here. I can't seem to ignore them. Every boom seems like a bomb, every crack a rifle shot, and so forth. Both Colin and I are so aware of every gun shot, machine gun fire, and other sound of violence. I don't remember this from my two previous visits here. It is so stressful to be able to hear it all. Why does it all have to happen? It is mostly people just trying to frighten each other and to show their power. At least that is what I want to believe.

I was wondering how many people get killed in all this show-off shooting and bombing. If someone kills me, I want them to know me, to see my face, know my name, what I do, and to think of my family and feel the consequences of the action. I don't want to die by the indiscriminate hand of a terrorist who kills anybody, just for some abstract idea or principle. I suppose it is easier, if that is possible, to kill a stranger who may represent some abstract cause, than to hurt someone you know. May God teach us to love in Lebanon.

Tuesday, June 1, 1982

Early in the morning

It's breakfast time. It is also the day on which our new pastor comes to town back there. I thought about our pastor leaving and a new one coming a lot yesterday, and it makes me both anxious and sad. I wrote the new pastor a note of welcome and wished him a good time during his adjustment to our small town.

Yesterday was Memorial Day there; I realized that too. Big deal! Colin told me yesterday was a bank holiday in Britain too.

Did I write that I slept in one of Nadim's one-year-old child's beds? He had made twin beds for the kids with high sides, but built on the floor. It was what he had to offer. It was fun but I had to remove all the toys first, before I could fit into it.

On previous trips to Lebanon I had worn my suits to work every day, or at least a tie. But on this trip I am being more casual; sometimes I dress up, but not regularly. Not everyone else does, and it is not my style anyway. Besides I should be relaxed just as suggested in the letter my family tucked in my bag for discovery on this trip.

Breakfast has arrived. By now there is a clear pattern to it. Every other day we have croissants, butter and jams; the other days it is eggs and toast, with an occasional rasher of bacon. Of course, we have a half grapefruit every morning. We've also decided that the evening meals are cyclic with a cycle of

one week. So we can expect the same thing tonight as one
week ago. We'll see.

I'm giving my exam now as I write. I've just been writing
a letter again. I'm going to spend today grading papers and
that will be a real chore.

Letter home
June 1, 1982, 7:20 a.m., Tuesday, Marquand House: AUB

Dear all,

*I wrote you Saturday and Luigi carried it to Italy to mail. You'll
probably get that letter before the others. But here comes another anyway.
I ought to be darned near home by the time this one arrives. That is a
strange thought, since I'm not even half way into my work here.*

*I am continuing to take the advice, which you wrote me in my note
about relaxing and enjoying myself. I'm having a peaceful time and not
working a lot like I did on the previous trips. Indeed, I do nothing,
except teach and prepare my lectures. Both Nabil and I realize that I'll
not be back any time soon, if at all, so there is no point to work on projects
which I cannot continue to complete.*

*I am well. I miss you all a lot, but seem to accept it and go on. I
want to come home and I'm already plotting how to end class a day early.
The students would like that and so would I. If I can leave early, I will
catch a Thursday flight and head out. Of course, I'll then have the dilemma
of whether to stay an extra day or lay over in Europe a night. If I go
through London, I won't be tempted to stay, but another city?? Maybe.*

*On Saturday I went to Jbiel, which is up the coast about forty or
more kilometers. It is the site of Biblos (from which the word "bible"
comes; the city was named for its parchment industry or "biblos" industry.)
It is considered the oldest city in the world. It is on the coast and there
are archeological ruins everywhere. From the man-made port, looking
like an old castle jutting out to the sea, to the French crusaders' castle on
the edge of a cliff over the sea, it is a wonderland of Middle Eastern*

*history. One of the students drove me and we toured a Frankish crusaders'
castle, the ruins of a Roman temple and amphitheater, and a Phoenician
burial grounds for royalty - all on the same area of land. The Crusader
castle was magnificent, although partly in disrepair. It was a labyrinth
of cubicles and stairs and turrets. All about it were the remains of a
thousand-year-old village enclosed in a great wall. I was quite amazed
by the largeness of the structure and wondered how it could have been
built way back then.*

*On Sunday I went up to Brummana in the mountains and about
twenty miles northeast of Beirut. It is an old resort town full of cafes
on narrow streets overlooking the valleys. The town is on top of a mountain
and we wound back and forth up the mountainside. I went at eleven
o'clock with Dr. Nabil Karam to visit him and his wife and children for
a day. We had a nice time; it was quiet and relaxing there, then we
returned on Monday morning early. They live very austerely with little
furniture or comforts. They are putting all they have into a medical clinic
and office for their practices. They took me to a Byzantine Catholic
wedding in East Beirut and it was a bore because we got there late and
missed much of the show. It was outlandish and gaudy - more than you
can imagine. Can you believe a camera crew with lights all over the
church, distracting everyone and moving all about the priest and couple,
looking for better and better shots?! Yes, it's true, and more, much more.
It was a good experience for me to see.*

*On Sunday evening we returned to Nadim's place in Brummana
and he visited a couple of patients while Huda and I worked on the clinic.
They plan to open this week and there is still lots of work to do. We
unpacked and shelved forms, put cabinets together and I varnished some
furniture too. I was exhausted but felt pleased to be of help.*

*On Monday morning we got up early to return to Beirut before the
early morning traffic jams. But there was a freak rainstorm at 5:45
a.m. and the roads down the mountain were slippery. Also, everyone left
early so we encountered bad traffic and the trip took two hours. There
was another rain and hail storm just as we got to AUB, and I got soaked*

and wound up standing under a porch for a while to keep out of the rain.

Gardenias are in season here. They are wonderfully fragrant and very strong smelling. People set them in a bowl of water and it scents the whole room. Also, it is common to see a girl with one on a string around her neck. It wilts quickly, but continues to smell sweetly, I guess.

Today I'm giving a quiz, then afterward I'm going to see Mr. Elie Nasr to select some souvenirs for you all back home. I intend to be more conservative in my purchasing on this trip. I've spent too much already.

I am really tired of this and want to come home. I think that I've finally gotten this Lebanon thing out of my system. I have not enjoyed this work nor have I minded it. But it seems to be a waste of my time. I must be here for a reason, I guess, but I surely can't guess what it is so far.

Hope you are happy and doing well while I'm gone. I am eager to be with you all .... I love you all dearly and look forward to our being back together again.

Chuck and Daddy

11:30 a.m.

I have returned to the house to work on my exams in peace. I stopped at my office after class and Nadim wanted to talk, so we went for coffee. Then we walked to a pharmacy and got some cream for my itch. We stopped at the jeweler E. Nsair's and I picked out gifts for all. I was careful in my purchases and bought nothing for myself. The girls will like what I have chosen, I am quite sure. I got gold snake-chain chokers for each of them. They will have to save them until they are older, I think, especially the two younger ones. I do not think they should wear 18-carat gold yet.

There has been a lot of fighting and shooting here in town since last night. I hear the grenades now as I write. It started last evening and continued until a while ago. Then it stopped. It sounds like it has started up again. When I went to bed last night, I was sure I could hear the fighting, but I thought I was just imagining it. That was what I wanted to believe too. But I could still hear it when I got up. By then Colin had checked it out at breakfast. Here is what I learned.

There are two radical groups about five minutes from here, and they are warring periodically, one is pro-Iranian and the other is a local communist group, we have been told. They shoot off guns, dynamite and use grenade propellers to ruin the buildings. It is crazy, but locally contained. The locals don't seem to hear it and they all walk along in sublime nonchalance. I don't know how much is noise and how much is real, but the dynamite and grenades have got to be doing something bad.

6:45 p.m.

I just got back from a neat little French Mass that I discovered. I've been so lonesome for church, and so much in need of a spiritual haven that I had to find one. As I started up the aisle, I was overwhelmed. But the time I got to my seat, I was nearly in tears. It's like the tears that will come when I see my family at the airport after this absence. I feel at peace tonight.

There is a cocktail party here at Marquand House on the first floor and the patio tonight. So I am stuck in my room until at least eight. Then we will have a late supper. Maybe Mohammed will let us eat leftovers from the cocktail party buffet. I saw it earlier before the guests arrived and it was beautiful.

I am reading some of Merton again today. It gives me some good thoughts, albeit for a short time.

The guests just hit the buffet table; I can hear them. Lucky guests!

10:45 p.m.

I'm off to bed, but I wanted to write a line or two first.

Colin and I chatted while the cocktail party went on. Then we headed down and made a feast of the leftovers. There was Lebanese food like kibbeh, hummos, shish tawook, etc., as well as salmon, deviled eggs, and caviar. I had two plates of goodies, plus fruit and coffee. Colin and I have been b.s.-ing ever since. We talked about nothing but it was fun. We are both very lonely here.

We ate supper on the terrace with the acting president of AUB, Dr. David Dodge. He is an American and was very pleasant to talk with. He has just arrived, and the party must have been for him.

Wednesday, June 2, 1982

I got up early and read a bit. Then I had some breakfast of soft-boiled eggs and toast. I walked up to the church where I had been last evening because I thought there was an 8:00 a.m. Mass. That was what their sign indicated, anyway. But there was not. It was an old sign. When I got to the office, I was locked out again, so I came back here to get ready for class. I think I'll also organize myself for my trip home now. If I can get it figured out, I'll be able to take all of my preferences to the AUB travel office and select a flight accordingly.

I want to run today before I eat lunch. I'm going to Raymond's home for supper and can't run later today. (I think his last name is Hayak, and he is related to a past government leader here, a minister of health, I think.)

2:20 p.m.

I'm having my coffee in the living room after lunch. I've got to get over to the office as I have to maintain hours there. But I'm late today since I ran.

My class went okay. The students chattered a lot and it bothered me. So finally today I stopped and told them how rude it would be considered if such behavior occurred in my American classroom. That worked. I forgave them by implication due to their different culture, but I did let them know how I felt about it too.

Last night at church I was captivated by a strange lady sitting in front of a life-sized statue of Jesus. She was talking to the statue dramatically and with lots of gestures. She repeatedly harangued the statue, by shaking her head and repeating her pleas and prayers. I could hardly take my eyes off her at first because she was so dramatic. I am glad I could not hear what she was saying, even though it was probably in French or Arabic. I just thought to myself, the poor lady is crazy and needs her "downers" strengthened. Well, today I walked across campus to see AUB's business manager who will do the flight tickets for me - and guess who? Yep, the crazy lady is the business office manager. She said to me, "Did I see you at prayer last night?"

I had a lovely lunch, not what I would have normally had. Colin ate at one o'clock, as we usually do, and I saw he had a nice pasta soup and sardine sandwiches. Well, I was hungry, but not hungry enough to eat a ground sardine sandwich. So I told Mohammed I'd eat after I showered, and could I just have some bread and butter, but no sandwich. Well, he decided I meant bread and butter, etc., but not made up as sandwiches. So he brought me a plate of goat cheese, sliced meats, fresh vegetables, pickles and olives, besides the bread and butter. It was so delicious, and so pretty. And I was spared the sardines without insulting Mohammed (who is very proud about his excellent food and his cooking skills).

I guess I had better get to the office now. I probably will not write until I return tomorrow morning. Raymond's wife has prepared a mezza, by the way. That is a many-dish meal, with great variety of foods, but only a little of each one. Let's hope there is no raw lamb or strange organ meats.

11:00 p.m., somewhere near Junieh

I am at Raymond and Paula's home near Beirut. It is in the eastern area, and so it is clean and lovely. We are actually up in the mountains somewhere.

We left Beirut at 3:30 and stopped in East Beirut to visit his mother. Then we drove up here. We visited his wife's father next door, a very wealthy and self-made man. He retired to here to run a produce plot and he seems to do that quite well. His gardens are magnificent, and he makes the most efficient use of a small amount of land. We ate raw almonds, plums, oranges, lemons, strawberries and vegetables as we walked about the small plots on the steep slopes.

Then we went to see a 300-year-old Lebanese mountain villa, a series of small houses about a paved garden, surrounded by a walled area of fruit trees. It was like a miniature medieval city, but with romantic charm.

We came back here for dinner and it was a great mezza, followed by the best of Lebanese sweet desserts. I made no pretext of shyness or allowed my recent weight gain to bother me. I ate and ate. I enjoyed it so much. There were some items new to me, like a thyme and onion dish, miniature hot sausages in oil, shawarma meat, and a garlic paste with mint leaves. Raymond's brother came, and later, his wife's mother and sister, and another couple from AUB. It was quite a delightful evening, all in all.

Their little girl Samer is 16 months old and so sweet and cute. I enjoyed her the very best of all.

They have invited me back for the weekend and I am tempted to accept at least for one day, if I can. It is so peaceful and nice here in the low mountains. It felt so good to walk in the garden and munch on fresh vegetables that I saw and picked myself.

This is another part of Lebanon that I've never seen; I am always in the center of Beirut where all the political crazies are.

This trip has been a real eye-opener in that I've seen so much of Lebanon that is not war-torn and full of tension. It is so reassuring to me.

The word I would choose for Lebanon is "pathetic" - such a crazy-quilt of human conditions. I wish my family and friends could be seeing this with me.

Thursday, June 3, 1982

8:20 a.m.

I got up early, shortly after five, to leave Raymond's home and come back here, but he overslept and we didn't leave until 6:30. But the traffic was light coming down the mountain and we were here shortly after seven. I went back to Marquand House, showered and had breakfast. Now I'm at the office and ready for class.

Today is the fourth anniversary of my move from Pennsylvania to Virginia, I think. Where has all the time gone?

Mr. Bitar called on me at Marquand House yesterday afternoon, but I was not there. His son is Khalil from the Medical College of Virginia back home. We met him twice at the Haddad home; they have a sweet little girl. I had carried a package from Kahlil to here when I came. I expect his father will now invite me to lunch.

11:00 a.m.

I taught my class and went to E. Nsair's to get my jewelry. I've come back home to read and write a while before I run. I have determined to run before lunch again because I really do prefer that time of the day. The only problem is my absence from the office. However, I came here to relax, just like I said earlier. So that is what I'm going to do. I'll go to the office after lunch.

I leave here in exactly one week, assuming my tickets are arranged as I have planned them.

I might get a letter from home today, if the post is working well. If one were mailed last Monday, today is the tenth day and I figured it would take eleven days for a letter to get here. However, Colin received a letter from Britain and it took eleven days.

There has been lots of shooting and booms again. I am sick of it. I still hear it every time but I'm losing interest in investigating it. That is a good sign of adjustment, I guess.

5:05 p.m.

I just got up from a half-hour nap. I am still so tired and sleepy. I was up late last night, and I just got up so early this morning too. So I'm exhausted, I guess.

Colin and I had a nice lunch together. His friend from the Qatar school at Brummana came and had fruit and coffee with us after lunch. We had a dish of chicken parts, cooked in tomatoes, onions, peppers and potatoes. It was a heavy meal for a lunch but it was tasty. I went back to the office afterward and said good-bye to Colin and his friend Eric Piper. Colin is going to spend the day and evening with him up there in Brummana and return in the morning. I am glad for Colin because this is his first time out of Beirut.

Tomorrow afternoon Colin is going to go to Syria with a friend. He will be treated grandly too, because his friend is wealthy and important. Colin is quite excited about it, as I would be also.

I worked with a student on her paper at the office this afternoon. Then I got a call that my airline ticket was ready, so I went and got it. I leave Thursday at 1:15 p.m. from here and go to Frankfort, West Germany. I arrive by six and stay until the next day at noon when I catch my flight home. I arrive at Dulles by 6:30 p.m. If someone is able to meet me right away, I will be home by nine.

I want to go to Mass at six again this evening. Mohammed just said that Mr. Bitar will be calling on me at 5:30 p.m. I wonder if I can still make it to Church.

I'm about to have supper in a back room on a tray because the President has called a special meeting here at Marquand House. All of the rooms are being painted except mine now, and they are meeting in mine. So here I am. I have learned that the meeting is to deal with a crisis in which a student has taken over the controller's office at AUB earlier today. I don't know any more but I'll find out what I can. I'm nosey, and the story sounds exciting.

Later ...

Here's a cute story I got today. Here in Lebanon you can tell the Catholic families from the Muslim ones by the number of children they have. Catholics have the smaller families, averaging 3+ children. It is the Muslims who have the larger families, say six to eight children, or even more. I learned that in Colin's demography lecture materials. They joke about Muslims having large families just like they joke about Catholics having the larger ones in the U.S.

I also learned that the student in the controller's office is angry about the awarding of scholarships; he thinks they are not being given out fairly. I think I will walk over to the controller's office after my coffee and see if there are lights on there, or if there is any action.

Colin was telling me that he has several cravings for special things that he cannot get here. I got to thinking about it too and I know what I want most of all, but it is not food. In the area of food I want a cup of real American coffee and a good cheeseburger with mayonnaise.

I wrote to both Paul and Ted earlier this week; I'll write Hayes today. I wanted to write to Russell too but I don't know his new address. I even wrote Brian a welcome letter. I love to write letters here, and have probably written more than twenty by now.

Friday, June 4, 1982

7:40 a.m.

I got up early and ran at six because of my planned trip to Sidon today. However, I spent much of the time running and thinking about Sidon, and I became very uncomfortable about it. I feel a real fear in going, like a foreboding voice telling me of danger. I want to cancel my going there due to this strong fear. But I would also love to see Sidon, Hariri Medical Center and Bassam's parents. I guess I'll have to decide soon. I just can't get over my sense of discomfort and danger in going there. While I was running, I said my prayers as I often do. Also, it was while I was praying that I had this continuous strange feeling about my going to Sidon.

Colin just joined me for breakfast. He came in from Brummana just now, and he has got to unpack, go teach, re-pack, and go to Syria for the weekend. I'm quite envious of him going to Damascus, but I'm looking forward to my own weekend here too.

Letter home

Friday, June 4, 1982 8:10 a.m. [Note: This letter was in a mail box in Beirut a long time, and arrived in the USA about six months later.]

Dear all,

I am ready to go to work, but I want to write you one more letter before I go. I'll probably be home before this letter arrives as I'll be there in eight days. I can't understand how the letter, which leaves today, can take longer than the person who leaves next Thursday.

I am supposed to go to Sidon today and I am torn between my desire to go there and my fear of going. For some reason (mostly because others have told me it is not safe all the time), I am scared to go there. But I really want to see Hariri Medical Center and Bassam Kawwass' family. I've got to decide in the next hour or so what I will do.

I got my ticket yesterday and I return by way of Frankfurt, leaving here on Thursday and arriving there on Friday evening. I'll cable you today so you'll know my plans. I hope you won't miss the final night of the novena because of me; I can wait in Dulles until you can arrive.

I've lost what little interest I had in this trip yesterday when my ticket home arrived. Already I am thinking about packing and getting ready to come home. I don't know why I came actually, except for the sense of obligation that I felt. It's certainly been a drudge and disappointing experience professionally. I wish I could have stayed home. If there is a reason, or a purpose served by this trip, I can't imagine what it is. Maybe I'll know when I get home.

I have no plans for this weekend. Several people have suggested to me that I go to the shore or the mountains, etc., but no one has actually followed up with a direct invitation. A Mr. Bitar has been trying to contact me, and I think he's going to invite me out, but I don't know if I'll be invited for a lunch or for a day this weekend.

The girls will be out of school next week, the day I return. We can start to plan some nice time together. I look forward to a good summer. Which reminds me, how is my garden?

I love you all.

Chuck and Daddy

10:25 p.m.

I decided to cancel my Sidon trip. It isn't that important, so why go? I've also heard that the Israeli ambassador to Britain was shot this morning in London and we are expecting some kind of a retaliatory attack soon on Lebanon - somewhere near the group which is responsible for the shooting.

I walked on Bliss Street earlier and bought a manooshe. (That is singular for mana-eesh, I learned.)

The University scene near my office. It would soon change.

3:25 p.m.

I rescheduled my office hours for this afternoon at three because I canceled my trip to Sidon, due to my unexplained fear. I told everyone that the students wanted more office hours with me.

I was going to write home about fifteen minutes ago but the excitement started. Jets came buzzing low over the city and the ground forces opened fire with missiles. In order to confuse the missiles, the jets let out hot air balloons from the jets. The ground-fired missiles hit the balloons. It appears that the big silver and red balloons are some kind of metallic decoys. The sights and sounds of this are dramatic - planes buzzing low, guns firing, balloons exploding full of smoke, and silence on the ground as all traffic is stopped. We assume that the Israeli ambassador has died and that the Israelis are retaliating. Boy, I am glad I am not in Sidon; it may be quiet there, but I doubt it, if it is not quiet here.

Later, during a moment of silence

They have flown over three times now, and we heard that the airport has been bombed. There is shrapnel falling from the anti-aircraft missies that explode in the air. I have a piece of shrapnel and I'll bring it home for all to see. It fell on our building and we picked it up after it cooled. It fell only a few meters from here. Here they come again. There are lots of ambulances now. God help all of us.

Five minutes later.

We are watching the action out of the window; a branch was just cut off by a bullet three meters from my face. I'm frightened.

Later ...

We had to evacuate that room as the shrapnel and bullets were falling there at the windows. Attack number four has just ended.

I hope that it quits. I don't want to stay here all night, but I can't go out so long as all the bullets and shrapnel are falling all over. God, please help all those people out there who don't have an AUB in which to hide.

Here comes attack number five.

Many of the students are frightened; some are crying. This

isn't just a small attack, like happens so often over Beirut. This is the real thing, everyone is saying. Everyone seems to know it too. 6:40 p.m., back at Marquand House

The attacks stopped at 4:50 p.m. I had walked back to Marquand House quickly between the last two shells. I just couldn't stand it to stay in that building and it seemed like the shells were becoming predictable, with three-to-five minute intervals. So I ran home. When it was all clear, I walked up town to see the people. There was a lot of shooting into the air, and ambulances and cars of wounded, honking their horns and racing into the American University Hospital. I was drawn to that area. Lots of people with machine guns, mostly teenagers, were shooting into the air to scare cars away from the main roads to the hospital so that they could get through to the emergency room.

The airport was hit. We've heard various and conflicting reports from the radio stations.

I am feeling great stress and tension. I thought that I would cry twice and didn't or couldn't. I went to the six o'clock Mass and prayed. As I entered the Church of Saint Francis Assisi, I noticed the sign over the door: Pax et Bonum. Outside of the church was the sound of ambulances and guns; it was a stark contrast to the quiet church with its few older ladies murmuring in French.

Now I know why I did not go to Sidon, and why I had that funny feeling and fear this morning while doing my prayers on the green field. We've heard it on the news - they've bombed lots in the south and in that area where I would have traveled today. There is much shooting nearby!

9:50 p.m.

I just got back from walking Jerius Khuri home and the night is so quiet. There are no cars, and no night sounds at all.

It is eerie. I guess it will be a day until life comes back to us.

Jerius Khuri is a blind, 26-year-old AUB graduate who has been hired by the university to translate both Arabic and English into Braille for the blind students and others. He has been using the den downstairs in Marquand House this year for his work area, and I have met him briefly once before. He got stuck here late today due to the bombings and so I invited him to supper with me. He is a bright man, sensitive and honest, and we talked for the past two hours as we ate. It took my mind off things quite well. I was pleased for some company too.

I heard an airplane in the distance. It was an Israeli bomber, I thought. I'll be hearing every plane and every loud sound for a while.

The airport is open again, we heard. There are estimates of 250 to 300 casualties including the dead, which are considered less than 40 or 50, they think. It will be some time, if ever, before they know. The Palestinians have been bombing in northern Israel from their ground positions in southern Lebanon tonight, we have heard on the radio.

I can't believe that I didn't go down the road to Sidon today, nor the weird feelings, unexplainable, that just wouldn't let me go. Did I experience some kind of premonition today? If so, why?

What will the people back home hear about the attack on Beirut and southern Lebanon today? Although it was late afternoon, it was midmorning there. They will hear it on the evening news in a few hours. I'll be asleep here as it will be nighttime here by then. I hope that they are not upset and can just trust in my safety.

I will never forget how we all ran to the doors and windows to see the display, the fireworks of war, like children at the fourth of July. And we returned for every attack, it seemed, even though we had to run inside when we saw and heard shrapnel and bullets hitting around us. What is it about us that drew us to watch, to risk our safety?

Did I tell you that I did student advising between the attacks, until it was not safe to stay near the windows of my office? And until no one was interested in trying to work anyway, once the reality of it set in. But for a time, life just went on. Everyone assumed that they knew exactly what and when to bomb, and it wouldn't be AUB or its environs. So people tried to conduct business as usual if they could. Few could today.

A letter from Paul M, Ashland, VA, which arrived in Beirut June 4, 1982

5-24-82

Dear Chuck,

I was really disappointed that I missed you before you went away. But as true Christians we have a common bond in our spirituality. Even though you are very far away, I feel very close.

Josie did a wonderful job on the liturgy on Sunday and really made a very spiritual closing for a successful year. I had a lovely day with Elizabeth at Marriottsville yesterday. It was nice to take time out and reflect.

I hope and pray that things are working out for you. I am looking forward to your return.

Your experiences of this war-torn country are, I know, going to be very valuable to us in our growth as true Christians.

Love you,
    Your brother in Christ,
        Paul

Saturday, June 5, 1982

6:00 a.m.

I awakened early and lay there until 5:20 a.m. before I got up and dressed quickly and came down quietly to the patio to meditate and to read. As it is, both Mohammed and Hassan are up and so, before I went out, a breakfast appeared.

There were some anti-aircraft missile booms already before six, maybe a half dozen. I suppose that it is just for show. It is still quiet this morning but I can hear some traffic, so it will be a bustling day later on, no doubt. I'm nervous with each sound I hear, however; not for my safety but for having to witness the things that may follow.

The radio reported only 30+ dead at the hospitals and about 150 casualties too. Hassan says that is only at the hospitals and a crude guess.

6:20 a.m.

Just finished the breakfast of poached eggs and toast. How wonderful it can be to be served breakfast with no fuss or work. I could easily get used to having a house staff.

I still cannot stop thinking about the circumstances that kept me from going to Sidon yesterday. It could only have been the result of many prayers for my safety.

6:30 a.m.

For some reasons I am crying finally. Tension from yesterday, I guess. Now, I'll forget about it.

7:00 a.m.

This is getting to be a continuing saga. We just had one (or more?) jets fly over and the missiles started. Then there was a pause, and it started again just as the roar of the jets became audible. Probably it is just a show of force, after the Palestinian shelling of northern Israel during the night.

In all of the excitement of yesterday, I don't think I wrote that I got three letters, two from home and one from Paul. It took them ten days to get here. They were most welcome too.

Thanks. I wrote several letters too in the morning; I wonder if they can go out with the bombing.

A letter to a friend in Virginia (It arrived there on October 20, 1982.)

Marquand House, AUB
Beirut, Lebanon
Saturday, June 5, 1982
7:30 a.m.

Dear Roger,

I've been up for several hours and am sitting on the veranda in the garden and enjoying the sea breezes. It is a beautiful morning here. I had my breakfast out here on a tray about 6:00. I'm staying here at the AUB president's home (mansion), a 103-year-old home. There is no AUB president until July 1, so I'm using his house and staff as a visiting professor; there is another guest too from London.

As beautiful as it is this morning, we've already had an Israeli jet raid over the Beirut area with its shooting, anti-aircraft missiles, etc. But I don't think they bombed. They were just showing force after Palestine's ground shelling of Israel last night, which was, in turn, a retaliation for the 1.5 hours bombing of Beirut which began yesterday afternoon at 3:20. Roger, you cannot imagine what it is like to watch the planes coming over, again and again, dropping their bombs, while the anti-aircraft missiles and ground fire shoot away at them. It creates a lot of debris in the air, even far away from the action, so that bullets and shrapnel fall all over. One large piece of lead from a shell fell about six meters from me and I've gotten it as a memento. Another piece ripped through a bush only three meters from my face and the leaves were torn up. It was frightening to watch the fighting and see all the bits of metal bouncing on the ground about the building. Of course, we went to the inside rooms of the building when this occurred.

I am well and have had a good time of my work here. I teach second-year masters students for two hours each day. I have one more week, then

I'll be home. I don't plan to visit in Europe at all, as I'm eager to come home. After this trip, I think that I've gotten the wanderlust out of my system. I've had a really maturing experience here, due to the "hotness" of the political situation and the military and terrorism here. I jump with every noise, it seems, and am conscious of all the sounds of fighting (e.g., I've heard about five large guns go off in the distance since starting this letter). But I feel safe, so long as I stay in this neutral area of AUB.

I've used the time to do some reflecting and I think I will make plans to leave MCV. I have two tentative jobs lined up for consideration this fall, and I'd like to have another one make an offer.... We'll see. I do pray about it a lot. I guess I really want to have a change....

Please give my warm regards to everyone and tell them how I'm looking forward to seeing them soon. I'll be in my office on Monday, June 14. Probably this letter won't have arrived to you yet.

I appreciate any prayers for my safety. Yesterday I was to be in the area of the bombing but wasn't. Would you believe that the reason was that I had a terrible premonition of danger and so didn't go? The power of prayers, I think.

See you soon.

Chuck

2:00 p.m.

I got tired of the war, so stopped writing this morning. I went out and sat on a park bench and read Merton a bit. Then I walked through town for a while. I saw a pair of casual shoes for one hundred Lebanese lira that I liked, but I don't need them so I didn't get them. I came back and decided to write awhile about my experience from yesterday. There is something therapeutic about the writing process.

[Note to the reader: What I wrote is a short story. I thought it would make a nice publishable article. I never published it until I prepared my earlier book Born in Beirut: A Priesthood, where it can be found on pp. 7-8. Here it is once more.]

I am sitting on the terrace of the beautiful 103-year-old presidential home on the campus of the American University of Beirut, Lebanon. This is my temporary home for three weeks. It's midmorning here, a cloudless 75-degree day, and I'm enjoying the sea breezes that are ever-present. Hassan [house staff] will soon bring me a pot of tea and I'll relax and pretend I'm in a Mediterranean wonderland. And I am, except for the non-visible sounds of the warring, the ground fire, the anti-aircraft missiles with their booming thuds, and the slightly quickened pulse inside me that has not diminished since the air attack on Beirut yesterday.

What am I doing here, a visiting professor to this most beautiful campus in this war-torn land? Am I really teaching graduate students health planning and policy, inspiring young minds to build a better Lebanon? I feel like the little girl Dorothy who has landed in Oz today; can I click my heels together three times, say, "Take me back to Ashland [Virginia]," and really be home?

My tea has arrived, so let me strain a cup, twist the lemon, and I'll tell you my story.

This is my third trip to Beirut. On each occasion, I have wanted to travel south sixty kilometers along the coast to Sidon, but it is near the "war zone." On both of my previous trips, my plans to visit Sidon were cut short by fighting in or near the city so that an American could not go there safely. (Nor could most anyone else, I suspect.) I had made up my mind to go this time. One of my students agreed to take me and the arrangements were made for a Friday departure at noon. That was the plan for yesterday - an afternoon in Sidon, with the return to Beirut in the late afternoon, to be home safely before dusk when safety exists no more.

I awakened early Friday in order to do all my daily regimens and prepare for work before I headed for the office and my morning of teaching. I headed first to the athletic "green field" at 5:45 a.m. for my daily 5.3 miles around and around the track. And, while running, I said my daily prayers. I had some trouble concentrating on the prayers, and keeping a correct count of the number of laps I'd run, because of a sudden fear of going to Sidon. I was scared. I felt a foreboding danger associated with the trip, but there was no justification for the feeling. By the time my run was over, I felt tense and confused; on the one hand, I wanted to go to Sidon to visit my associates, but, on the other, I felt this uncomfortable way. Was I being "told" not to go, or was I a bit neurotic? I couldn't decide. At breakfast I decided to forget it all, to simply confront the student-driver at 10:30 and when I had to, to make a snap judgment about the trip.

I decided that I had better listen to my feelings and I didn't go. The student was concerned; he knew I was fearful, although I told him a lie about another unexpected appointment, which had come up.

At my class later in the morning I announced that I would, after all, keep my afternoon office hours from 2:00 to 4:00 p.m. Appointments were made for 3:00 and 3:30. I went to lunch with the student-driver; he hoped I was enjoying Lebanon and wasn't getting nervous being here. I wasn't nervous, but I knew what I could not do.

I walked on Bliss Street earlier and bought a manooshe for lunch. Can't get enough of them.

My first appointment at three was brief and Mrs. Topjein, my secretary, came in. I could not hear her well for the sounds of an airplane. AUB is on a landing course for the international airport; when planes come over, one cannot hear. The explosions began at 3:20. Then I realized that the noise was not that of a passenger jet landing at the airport. I was not afraid, just annoyed. Being here, one gets used to the sounds of guns, bangs and booms. This seemed like just some more of the regular daily dose of violence. But it wasn't.

I was going to write you a few minutes ago, but the excitement started. Jets came buzzing low over the city and the ground forces opened fire with missiles. In order to confuse the missiles, the jets let out hot air balloons from the jets. The ground missiles hit the balloons. It appears that the big silver and red balloons are some kind of metallic decoys. The sights and sounds of it are dramatic - planes buzzing low, guns firing, balloons exploding full of smoke, and silence on the ground as all traffic is stopped. We assume that some ambassador has died and that this is some form of retaliation. Boy, I'm glad I am not in Sidon; it may be quiet there, but I doubt it, if it is not quiet here.

The students congregated in the great stone arch of the building's portico to watch the attack. They sent Haytham to fetch me. "Professor, come and see the show," he called and tugged my arm. Just in case the planes made only one pass, he wanted to be sure that I saw the action.

Standing with the students, I felt anxious. Some were clearly frightened, but others seemed exhilarated by the excitement of what was to come. When I looked up into the direction of their pointing arms, I saw first the metallic hot air balloons as they floated downward then were hit by the anti-aircraft missiles, and exploded in a cloud of smoke.

They pointed to the planes, but I couldn't see them. The ground fire was deafening. Then it ended.

We were edgy, but it had been a good show. Sima [my student appointment] ran into the courtyard in front of us; she'd seen a bullet hit. Dear Sima, she's quite scared, and after living through all these war years too!

The next attack came about three minutes later. More of the same. "Don't worry, Professor. It's to be expected. Figure ten, maybe even twenty minutes." Interest waned, and people returned to find radios. A half-hour later and on the seventh or eighth pass, interest was high again. It had been too long. "Why don't they stop?" Listen to all the ambulances coming to AUB's nearby medical center. As we assembled at the portico once again, shrapnel began to fall. A big piece of an anti-aircraft missile hit about five meters from me and slid into the culvert along the building entrance. My reaction was direct and immediate - I wanted it as a souvenir. "Wait til it cools and the attack is over." I had it in my hand in five more minutes, a piece of steel the size and shape of my little finger, clearly a lethal weapon if it should fall on a person. Everyone wanted to see it, our human and macabre curiosity. When more pieces fell, the status of my piece of shrapnel decreased.

The rain of shrapnel forced us inside the building completely, but our fascination led us to hand out the ground floor windows to watch the next attack. I jumped suddenly as the leaves on the branch outside the window (and less that three meters from my face) were shredded by falling debris.

Enough is enough. The windows were closed, and everyone retired to the inner hall.

During a five-minute pause between the next two attacks, I met with my 3:30 appointment. Why not, it seemed. A quick meeting though, as we couldn't stay in my office due to the large windows. I started to wonder if we'd be stuck in this building all night. I was, however, grateful that we were in this safe part of the city. We didn't know how much damage was being done, but we were glad we were not in the areas of the Palestinians. Surely there was some real damage.

Suddenly I had to get out of there. I wasn't afraid of falling shrapnel or bullets. When the next attack ended, I took off across campus for my lovely residence at the presidential house overlooking the sea. I arrived safely, despite the student's dire predictions to the contrary. There was another brief attack, during which time I was busy showing off my shrapnel to the house staff. That was the end of it for Friday, June 4; it was 4:50 p.m. The silence, which came over the city, was deafening and more frightening than the war sounds. Shortly the sounds of ambulances, car horns, and rifle and machine gun fire relieved us from the silence.

I hurried out of the campus gates and into the city. Many men could be seen with machine guns, mostly boys, teenaged and excited. Periodic bursts of gunfire warned motorists to stay away from streets where ambulances or cars of wounded would be coming. Fear and tension filled the air. All the shops were closed and bolted with metal coverings. There was little of the normally heavy Friday afternoon traffic. I walked uptown to see the people. I was drawn to the area of the American University Hospital. Lots of people were shooting into the air to scare cars away from the main road to the hospital so that people can get through to the emergency room.

The airport was hit. I've heard various and conflicting reports from the radio stations. I am feeling great stress and tension. I thought I would cry twice and didn't or couldn't. I wanted to go to Mass and pray.

I continued up the street past the boys with their old machine guns and gleeful expressions. On Hamra Street, I turned left and entered the Church of Saint Francis where there was an evening Mass. Over the door was carved "Pax et Bonum." It was 6:00 p.m. and time for daily Mass. Outside the church were the sounds of ambulances and guns; it was a stark contrast to the quiet church with its few older ladies murmuring in French.

[No priest came. A woman there told me that the area south of the city, particularly Sidon, had been badly bombed. I sat and cried. God had spoken to me, I now knew. But I wondered why.]

Well, I hadn't written long when Jerius came. He told me of massive shelling and fighting in the south of Lebanon. Once as we talked, we had to go inside due to the planes and shelling over southern Beirut. Then he asked me why I was going home right away on Thursday. When I told him I wanted to be home for my Sunday school class beginning on the following Sunday, his ears perked up. He had left church life years ago, very angrily, and now wanted to study philosophy, including Catholicism. But he feels he isn't good enough or holy enough, and he doesn't want to get that way either. We talked about the meaning of God, religion and church and about the problems of organized churches. It was a good discussion for both of us. Maybe he will now be more open to grow in himself.

Jerius and I had a nice lunch. Mohammed is tired and looks bad. I just learned why. His wife is in southern Lebanon in the middle of the area of shelling and fighting last night and this morning. She went there and tried to come back but got caught there. He has gone to lie down now. He is ill due to stress. There is no way to contact her to see if she is safe.

2:40 p.m.

More jets, more gunfire, lots and lots of ground fire. Nonstop for a couple of minutes. I have to head for cover for the fourth time today. Always a fear of shrapnel. Now the sound of an ambulance.

This is starting to get on my nerves.

7:30 p.m.

I finished writing my brief experiences from yesterday and I like it. It will be good to share with everyone back home. Then I lay down for a half hour before I ran. After I ran, I walked to town. I bought one of those crescent-shaped almond cookies from the French pastry shop. It is located near the hotel where I stayed two years ago, and I've enjoyed those cookies on each visit here. So I had to have one.

Then I walked to six o'clock Mass. I expected it to be in English but it was in French. It was also the Sunday service which I did not expect either.

The song "Be Not Afraid" is going through my head a lot today. There is a line in it which I catch on, "You shall travel far in safety." **In safety** (*Be Not Afraid.* Bob Duffold, S.J. and New Dawn Music, 1975).

Did I write that I quit shaving my cheeks when I came here? I'm going to let my beard grow in and then reshape it this summer.

Sunday, June 6, 1982

5:55 a.m. Marquand House

I went up to bed before eight last night and read a while, but turned out the light and went to sleep shortly thereafter. I was so tired that I went to sleep immediately. Consequently, I awoke about four this morning, but I catnapped until after five when I arose. I have been sitting on the patio since then meditating and reading, and having some coffee. Now my breakfast is here. I have a half grapefruit again, as nearly every morning. They are so sweet and juicy here; of course, they are fresh too. All the citrus fruits grow here, and almost year round.

Every morning I look out to the sea and it is so calm and extant. Each day there is a beautiful pattern of surface currents, which are never the same. The patterns can only be seen when the sun shines on them from low in the sky. So I can't see them during the day. In the evening, it is a bit misty or foggy so that they are difficult to see. This is the best time to experience their wonderful patterns.

I have an idea. When I get back home, let's clean up the patio and use it as a place for early morning quiet. Perhaps we could even breakfast there sometimes. We'd need a table and better chairs, but it is a lovely and serene place to be in the early morning - much like on the veranda of Marquand House. Starting the day in a calm and serene place has a relaxing effect on the whole day, I think.

Sunday, 6:20 a.m., June 6, 1982
Marquand House
American University of Beirut
Beirut, Lebanon

Dear Dan, Vada and James,
    I get a lot of my correspondence caught up when I'm traveling so please do not be too surprised by my letter. I awakened quite early again today, and have been sitting here in the garden of AUB's presidential home for about an hour now. I arrived here to teach a 3-week graduate course in public health about two weeks ago. I am occupying this vacant 103-year-old mansion since it will not be occupied by the new president until mid-July. It is a huge place overlooking the Sea and situated in the middle of the most beautiful university campus in the world. Mohammed served my breakfast here on the terrace by 6:00, so now I'm relaxing with a pot of coffee as I write to you. One would think I'm in a tropical wonderland to look about me and see the beautiful mansion, flowers, and nearby sea. And I am. Except for the invisible sounds of ground fire, missile thuds, and a quickening heartbeat that I have had ever since the air attack on Friday afternoon.

[Note: Between the time I have started this letter and now, I've heard about 100 gun shots, rifles and machine guns. It's mostly crazies looking for attention.]

I leave Thursday afternoon, and I've set a schedule with a stay-over in Frankfurt. I've never been in Germany so will look forward to a day there. Maybe I'll even get a chance to practice my German in the 21 hours that I will be there. I could stay an extra day, but I'm eager to get home after nearly three weeks.

It has been a politically "hot" time here this trip. And that converts into an equally hot time militarily. One my first morning here, the French embassy (about a quarter mile from campus) was bombed. Another day there were jets dog-fighting over the city and then Israelis shot down two Syrian "migs." Of course, I've lost count of all the ground skirmishes and miscellaneous bombs. One becomes quickly blase about the daily dose of violence.

Friday's attack was focused on the part of the city where there are Palestinian hide-outs, artillery stockpiles, etc. (I guess.). But the rain of debris - bullets and shrapnel - covered all the city. It started at 3:20 p.m. with the buzz and roar of the jets, then the deafening roar of the ground fire and anti-aircraft missiles. I was escorted to a large stone portico at the entrance to our building, so that I could watch the performance. They pointed out the planes, but all I could see were the metallic hot-air balloons (anti-aircraft missile decoys) which were released, floated along, then exploded int a could of smoke as the ground missiles struck them. The first attack was exciting, but with the second one, we retreated to find radios to see if they were bombing. They were. Then the shrapnel started to fall, and we had to retreat again. A large piece fell about five meters from me, and I got it as a memento when it cooled (and between the attacks). As we stood at the windows, more shrapnel and bullets whizzed by even closer, so we went to the inside corridor. Excitement became tension, even fear, among the Lebanese. So I knew that this was the real thing. When it stopped with the last pass over, it was ten minutes before five, and we were glad. Thank God were in a safe part of the city. However, the silence which came over the city afterwards was even *more deafening than the sounds of the war. Fortunately the ambulances and gunfire started up and relieved us of this silence.*

So what's up with you? Will we see you come this way this summer? Where will your vacation be spent? We have planned a week at the ocean and several long weekends so far.

We hope all are well there. We are just fine. It will be the end of school on June 11 and we are looking forward to a very family-oriented summer.

> *Love,*
> *Chuck Breindel and family*

6:50 a.m., at breakfast

I just wrote Uncle Dan and Aunt Vada a letter. I always get correspondence caught up when I am away (even if sometimes I cannot post it until I get home).

I was just thinking about the news reports back home. They must have covered the bombing of Beirut and southern Lebanon, and the subsequent day of bombing and fighting south of here. They must have heard of it. I could call them to let them know I am fine, but if they have not heard much, then that will only be a bit disturbing for them. I'll just hope that they know I am safe and well, if they know there is trouble here.

10:50 a.m.

I went to 7:30 church and it was in French again. They do have services in Arabic and in English, but I have not managed to get to one of these yet. Then I came back here, changed and ran. When I got back to Marquand House I learned that Eva Jarawan had called to invite me to lunch with her, Salim and Ria at noon. I showered and read the paper in my room while munching on the half kilo of jumbo cashews, which I bought Friday.

The report of Friday's bombing was very conservative and fair in the International Herald Tribune. It gave no suggestion of the problems where I am. If that is all that was reported in the U.S., then I am greatly relieved. They will not be worried about me if they read something like that.

11:10 a.m.

Two large bombs just went off and the house shook. Something is happening. We heard that two planes were downed and at least one of the pilots is dead. This will mean more fighting.

11:40 a.m.

A MEA passenger jet was flying overhead as an Israeli jet flew higher overhead. The people on the ground opened fire on the jet and I held my breath for the other plane. I guess that they know what they are doing, but it certainly looks bad from the ground for the MEA jet.

I wonder how many different types of flowers there are on the trees, bushes and plants of AUB campus. I started to count them but quit at ten. But there are many more. It is really the flowers and trees that help to make AUB a beautiful place. Of course, the beautiful steep hills to the sea help too.

3:45 p.m.

Sunday in Beirut, the day for promenades and strolling along the corniche. Everyone comes out and walks. I've told you about this social phenomenon before. Not today though. There is hardly a soul out, except maybe a few with portable radios. Everyone is at home with the news on.

The corniche along the sea is deserted on Sunday morning.

It is a sad day for Lebanon. Their worst fears seem confirmed. Israel has finally decided to take the southern part of Lebanon. Eva and Salim had me come for dinner. They said, "We knew you would not want to be alone on this day."

There is an all-out attack on southern Lebanon. Israel is bombing and has sent ground forces. Our dinner would have been lovely, with Salim's two brothers and two sisters, except the radios and TV were on constantly, as each new moment of news came. President Reagan has said he will evacuate us Americans if the Israelis move too far north. But no one thinks they will go beyond Sidon, although some think they will eventually come to Damour, about eight miles south of here. If they should do this, we will have to leave Beirut. But it won't happen.

Salim jokingly suggested that I keep all of my valuables together in one place in order to grab them quickly. However, in 1976 when the Americans were evacuated from here, they had lots of advance notice.

The airport is still open here. We can hear the war occasionally, despite the great distance.

The highway to Sidon was totally devastated, so no traffic can move. And Sidon has been bombed repeatedly. I would never have gotten out of Sidon had I gone there on Friday. I can't believe that I didn't go, and how I came to stay here.

Salim said it will be very bloody fighting in the south. How can it be possible that we sit here in this beautiful Mediterranean area of AUB and there is a war so near? I am feeling very stressed by this. The fact that all the Lebanese people about me are scared and upset really bothers me. I know that they know the difference between war and the regular fighting. I wish I were going home tomorrow.

4:30 p.m.

I've had diarrhea for a couple of days. It is any wonder? I just wrote my final quiz for my class. I'll get it typed up tomorrow.

4:35 p.m.

I just received a phone call informing me that Americans are being advised to evacuate the country. It was from Nadim Karam, M.D., who heard it on the radio. I'm actually scared for the moment.

I called AUB security.

The announcement has been on the radio on two stations but not on the official radio station. We (Mohammed and I) are calling the American Embassy now. I guess someone would call me if it were true and so I'll try to relax and not overreact. I put that "Do not worry about tomorrow ..." card in my pocket. I'll read it too. Tell me, someone, what should I do if I have to evacuate? How does one evacuate?

5:25 p.m.

I called the U.S. Embassy and finally got through to a woman. She told me that the families of the Embassy staff are being evacuated first thing in the morning. They have all gotten airline tickets and will get out on the first flights. In addition, they are evacuating down to a skeleton crew. I asked for help, asked her to advise me, but she said she could tell me nothing. I asked her to tell me things off the record. She advised me to go. "Call some other Americans," she said, "and find out what they are doing and stay with them." She told me to try to get an airline ticket too and get out like they were doing. But I'm not able to get an airline ticket on a Sunday afternoon during a war. I'll have to wait until tomorrow and try. I asked her what to do if there was no airport by the time I got a ticket. I'm going to try to be slow to move. Perhaps I'll pack tonight, however.

We can hear the war off in the distance now. Deep thuds and booms. It's so very sad. You cannot know the ache I feel inside as I listen to all of this about me. About twenty minutes ago, there was much gunfire on the shore in front of us here. Mohammed went to the window and said he thought maybe the Israelis were landing here. My heart actually stopped for a moment until we learned it was a wedding party. (Gunfire is a traditional custom at some weddings here!)

I am like a cat on a hot tin roof.

A note on a small piece of lined white paper, given to me in Beirut so I could contact the American Consulate:

American

Consulate

direct line
Eva Haddad
369128

9:05 p.m. (after a phone call from home)

I just had your telephone call and it was good to hear your voice. I am sorry about the circumstances of your call, however. I would have telexed you tomorrow anyway. I didn't feel good after your call though.

Colin arrived back from Damascus at 5:40 p.m. and he had a wonderful trip. He had lots of stories for me which I enjoyed. Also, he calmed my nervousness with his presence. He hopes we don't get told to go, since he doesn't want to go. He thinks that, since the American Embassy is advising to leave, it is quite political. After all, the British, Canadian, French, etc. are not worried, or are at least not evacuating their embassies. I feel better now except for your phone call. I am upset more so that you are worried. I told you not to worry, that I would leave if they really told us to, or if there is any possible danger. But I don't think that you listened to me or believed me. (I did not believe myself either, since I don't think there is way to get out now.)

I wished that damned ticket of mine were clarified. I am angry that the flight arrangements were so screwed up that no one knew my plans. I'll clarify my flight arrangements tomorrow and I'll cable them home.

Well, I'm not nervous so much anymore, so I'll go to bed. Please relax and trust me and God.

Monday, June 7, 1982

6:55 a.m.

I awoke about four but stayed in bed for an hour. Then I

got up and ran on the green field at 5:45 a.m.

Now I am back, showered and at the breakfast table. I have not resolved what to do but it may have been resolved for me. I have heard none of the morning flights arriving. This means that the airport is closed and I cannot leave anyway. It may be just a temporary thing, however. I have got to spend my next few hours gathering the facts so I can learn my options.

10:00 a.m.

Classes are canceled and there is much tension all over the campus. The students are nervous. I am going home to Marquand House, I think. I will give my quiz tomorrow and then leave if I can.

I bought a manooshe and the streets were calm when I went out there. Indeed, they were peaceful, as it is south of Lebanon.

11:05 a.m.

I've heard two planes arrive so the airport must be open now. Maybe I'll get out of here tomorrow. I'll be ready.

I took my airline ticket to the business services office and told them to get me a ticket out of here tomorrow. They promised to try but don't know if the airport will be open. I said I would go to the port of Junieh by car and catch a boat to Cyprus if I couldn't fly. They will check that out too. (Others are saying that is the only way out.) If they can get me out, I'll have a ticket by the end of today, they promised.

Now I'll have to tell my boss Nabil about my decision to leave immediately, when he arrives later today. He will not be pleased, I expect. I'll have to use some of my recently acquired insight and not be too concerned about pleasing others. I need to do what I think is best.

I called together those students I could find and told them

to take my final exam tomorrow at 8:30 a.m., or else to produce their papers. I'll grade one or the other, I said. I can read them on the plane home, I guess.

I will cable home just as soon as I know any definite plans. I feel better now that I have made some distinct plans. I needed to do this.

We cannot hear the fighting much today, except when an Israeli jet comes over and the anti-aircraft guns fire up at them. It is relatively quiet, since all of the action is in the south.

Colin gave me some diarrhea medicine this morning at breakfast and it helped almost immediately.

A telex sent from AUB, Beirut to USA office for transmittal

June 7, 1982

TO BAJADA   FROM BREINDEL
PLS CALL MRS BREINDEL 804-798-6687
WILL DEPART BEIRUT ON EARLIEST POSSIBLE
FLIGHT TUESDAY.   HOPE TO ARRIVE USA ON
WEDNESDAY.   WILL CALL WHEN I ARRIVE.   I'M
FINE AND SAFE.   LOVE TO ALL.

12:30 p.m.
It will soon be lunch and I'm not hungry at all. I walked to town and bought some things I wanted for myself - a small bottle of aftershave lotion and a pair of brown clogs (I told of them already, I think.). I hadn't bought anything for myself on this trip, and I had determined to do so. But I did not want any jewelry like I got for everyone else.

I can hardly hear myself think for the music which is now blaring along the wall out by Marquand House. There is a rally of Palestinian students and they are blaring away their patriotic music and military chants on a loudspeaker system at full volume. Of course, no one is going to go out there and tell them to turn it down.

There was a lot of ground fire in the last fifteen minutes. There must be planes flying overhead nearby. As I write these words, it has escalated so that the house has been shaken by several booms. (I really want to get out of here, now that leaving is getting close to a reality.)

3:05 p.m., at Marquand House

This long day drags on and on. I just got a ticket for tomorrow's flight to Frankfurt. It is a lousy connection with a stop at JFK and then on to Washington National. I don't know if I'll be able to get out, however, because the situation is quite dangerous here and the airport is closed now. What good will a ticket do me if I can't get a flight out, due to no airport service? I am not getting my expectations too high, because it may be several days before I can get out. Even the port road is closed, so I can't get across to that place where there are boats to Cyprus.

The American Embassy was shot into with a couple of missiles about 2:00. I don't think there was a lot of damage but it was quite loud. It sits adjacent to AUB, in the area near my office. (I have learned that the two missiles went through the sixth floor of the American Embassy, but no one was injured.)

Nabil Kronfol returned from his trip to Bahrain at 2:00. I saw him briefly. He said how unfortunate that we won't get to work together. He said that because he thinks I expect him to say it. I know that and he knows that I know it.

I sent another cable home saying that I'd try to leave tomorrow and that I will call when I know how, when and where I am going. There is no point in sending a telex until I am sure that I can get out.

June 8, 1982

TO BAJADA   FROM BREINDEL
PLS CALL MRS BREINDEL (804-798-6687) GIVING
THIS MESSAGE FROM ME: "DEPARTURE FROM
BEIRUT NOT POSSIBLE AT THIS TIME. WILL LEAVE
AS SOON AS SAFE CONDITIONS. I AM SAFE AND
WILL CALL FROM EUROPE WHENEVER I GET
THERE. DO NOT WORRY, BUT CALL MY PARENTS.
CONTINUE PRAYERS AND RELAX. LOVE TO ALL."
THANKS.

5:00 p.m.

Bad news. An afternoon of Israeli jets and constant barrage of ground fire and missiles. All the while the fight songs of Palestinians roar through our house from next door. We watched a lot of the air action, especially the dog fights, with their appearance of red fireworks as they fired away.

Our house was hit by a pile of metal. We think there is a hole in the roof but haven't confirmed it yet.

The AUB president David Dodge called me to say he was sorry that the airport was closed and probably would remain so for some time. I'd be safe, he said, if I would just stay on AUB campus and indoors. He said the university will do their best to get me out of here someday soon, possibly by overland to Damascus, if the airport won't open. So now I'm supposed to sit still and have no expectations for leaving. I am safe if I stay still.

They bombed Beirut this afternoon, but I don't know much for sure. (It's true; the Arab University has been bombed.) The war has become quite real and close to me now. As of this afternoon, we are in it all and cannot get out. Like everybody else, I am glued to the radio, listening for news in English.

5:45 p.m.

We just discovered a huge hole in our roof and a bullet lodged in the ceiling of the bedroom beside Colin's room. We sent a little boy up into the attic and he pulled the bullet out. We flipped a coin for it and Colin won. But I got another one of the same type from Mohammed's son who found it outside. It is ugly.

7:00 p.m.

Another twenty minutes of Beirut bombing and it is quite beautiful to see the huge sprays of red, white and yellow lights from the ground with each pass overhead. The sounds are deafening but the spectacle of light is amazing.

8:45 p.m.

The war is over for Beirut for the day, although we know it is waging on most violently south of here. The war has gotten unexpectedly very close to us today. We hear that they are quite near us in an area about Damour and toward the airport but we can't confirm it.

There were long lines in town this morning and all the bakeries sold out. There were long lines at gas stations, as a result of the bombing and destruction of oil refineries in Lebanon last Friday and Saturday. It will be a frantic day tomorrow.

I wanted to go to six o'clock Mass tonight, but it was not considered safe to go out. Also the government has cut the electricity in town and all of Beirut is without electricity tonight (but not AUB as we have a generator of our own). There is fear of electric fires from all of the bombings so all the electricity has been cut, I guess.

The silence again tonight after the bombing of Beirut is fantastic. It is eerie and very frightening.

We heard on the 7:45 news that the United States may send a navy ship to get us out if we cannot get out. If there are no flights tomorrow, it is a good possibility. I would be thrilled to go any way, any time. The war has become far too real for me today. Although I am safe here, I cannot tolerate the noise and sights and shaking of the house during the day (or the silence right now). If the bombing did not stop or if it started up again, I'd have crawled out of my skin. I was so edgy.

I can't get over it! A Russian-made bullet broke a big hole in the roof and the bedroom ceiling! We could get killed here, not like the hundreds being blown apart near here, but nonetheless quite dead. Both Colin and I are amazed by all we are seeing. We are thinking what we will tell our children and grandchildren about this. (For now, get us out of here so we can think clearly.) We just had a loss of electricity for about a minute and it was terrifying.

Later ...

I've come to bed now and soon will greet another day of war. It may be the day of my departure, maybe by air. Or it could be my first sea voyage.

Tuesday, June 8, 1982

6:30 a.m.

The war began early here in Beirut on this Tuesday morning. I awoke at 4:20 with my case of diarrhea, so I meditated and got ready to run. It was a ghastly quiet morning until the planes came.

It was about 5:25 a.m. when they started. (Here they come again!) They came for twenty minutes to bomb Damour, about eight miles south of here, not far from the airport. It was rather distant for much excitement here. There was a family down on the green field at 5:15 a.m.; it was probably the family of a guard or worker at AUB who brought them here into the compound for safety. I wonder how much of a problem this will get to be. Already the city is receiving many refugees who are fleeing from the south. They are filling the parks, etc., after they have lost all they have.

I don't know if there will be classes or students today. I have no expectations, and I'll not get down if I can't get out. If I can't get out today, I'll try to call home to put them at ease. They must be very scared by now; I wish they could know how safe I am. I will not be upset if I can't get a plane or phone line either. There were no phone lines yesterday. Now for some breakfast.

There is no bread. Mohammed went for some at 6:00 a.m. and there were about five hundred people waiting in line already, he said.

6:40 a.m., and our second bombing wave already!

Now 7:35 a.m. and two more attacks south of here. The radio, both local and BBC, say the Israelis are heading for Beirut. I guess we should be nervous. We are, but not too much. They are still about a dozen miles south of here and moving.

8:45 a.m.

I'm at the office, but only three students made it and there are no classes. I'll grade those papers I have and call it quits. The administrative assistant called to wish me luck; they'll send a car if there is any chance of getting me to the airport this morning for my 11:30 flight.

None of my students could study last night due to the loss of electricity in Beirut. It was due to cables being cut south of Beirut at the war, they told me.

A letter to my prayer group back home (It was never mailed.)

Tuesday, June 8, 1982

9:45 a.m. (In my AUB office)

To my prayer group in Ashland:
I did better this week. Less organized prayer, but more prayerful thinking. Mass and Communion last week were so helpful. My joy at receiving Communion last Tuesday will be something I shall always remember.

The shelling last Friday confused me but led me to an acceptance of God in all of my life, even then and there.

When I didn't go to Sidon because of a foreboding feeling, I knew God was with me in a special way. My life maybe, and my safety certainly, were given to me as a result of God touching me. It was made possible by all of our prayers.

I've survived emotionally intact the events since last Friday. In my Christian eye, I've taken it all in, but cannot yet interpret its value to me. But I am closer to God in my spirit.

I helped Jerius Khuri question his religion, spirituality and gave him a touch of God's personal love for Him. He had a little spark inside of him, I think. Maybe it will glow again.

I have not given coins to the poor on the streets.

Mass and Communion are wonderful. I was disappointed that I couldn't go last night, due to the danger of the war. There was bombing at five and it renewed at seven.

Chuck

10:30 a.m.

Beirut was just bombed, I think. The jets are doing something south of the city too.

My diarrhea is quite terrible today.

I went over to the office at eight and several students showed up and gave me their papers to read. Two of the students never showed up. Also, because there was no electricity, they had difficulty doing their papers in the dark. Still, some tried!

Nabil came in and told me the airport has completely shut down (and the staff has left, I guess.) So I am packed and ready to go at 11:30 a.m., but I don't expect anyone to show up unless the airport should open quite suddenly. Nabil thinks we are here for a while. When I was walking back here to await possible departure, the Dean met me and said to be prepared for a Mediterranean cruise. (It is the local rumor that we will go out by ship, but it is not anything confirmed.) More realistically, it is expected we will be able to get to the airport on Thursday or Friday. We'll have to wait and see.

11:30 a.m.

No driver appeared now, no ride to the airport, no departure. Instead, an air raid and bombing on the area south of Beirut near the airport. They want me to know I cannot fly for sure.

2:00 p.m.

I read to my blind friend Jerius for an hour to take my mind off things. (I was dictating as he punched it out in Braille.) Then we both had lunch with Colin. Colin is busy looking for shrapnel about the lawn to keep and take back home as souvenirs. I received another big chunk from my students this morning from the campus.

I went to the travel office and heard some good news. We will be getting out of here tomorrow, along with the American Embassy people who stayed, if it can be arranged. They plan to car pool us (if there is no ground fighting at the border to the east side of Beirut) to Junieh, then put us on a boat to Cyprus to catch flights there. It sounds romantic, but I am told it is definitely not. We shall see. I won't get my hopes up. I didn't get a new plane reservation, as they didn't think the airport would open for a while, but Colin has one for tomorrow at 12:30 p.m., a London flight. And if he does go, I'll be with him!

The fighting is south of the city in the Damour area still, maybe twelve to fifteen miles away. The constant bombing and guns are always audible; it sounds like a perpetual low thunder. God help the locals. The carnage is terrible, we hear.

An area of Beirut that has been bombed.

8:42 p.m. (in bed)

It is hard not to be disappointed to be here still. I was really wanting out, although there was no chance at all. Also, my diarrhea has been so bad it has left me weak. Colin's pills are nearly gone and really don't seem to have much effect anymore.

I ignored the war today in my immense boredom. There were lots of booms and quakes as the war is so very close.

One sonic boom at about three this afternoon rattled the house in a way I cannot explain. I thought it would crumble. Poor blind Jerius was terror-stricken and tried to run from the windows, fearful of breaking glass. I took him to the hall and we went into the closet under the steps like frightened children. It must be ghastly for a blind person to hear all the sounds of war. His anger at God for his blindness came out again.

[Note to the reader: I did not record in the diary what happened under the stairs with Jerius. It is found in my earlier book though, and is reprinted here, as follows.]

I Want to See.

4th Sunday of Lent, A: Ephesians 5:8-14, John 9:1-41

Let's face it: The man-born-blind could not have received his sight any other way, except through the generous love of Jesus Christ. What is more, the blind man didn't ask for it. He didn't even know to ask, because he didn't recognize who Jesus was, at least not when it happened.

Nor did the blind man ask for the gift of his blindness either. Does that surprise you that I call blindness from birth a "gift"? It was. First, it was a gift to the man so that he might come to experience God's saving power through Jesus' miraculous cure. And it gave him the ability to know Jesus as the Messiah. Second, it was a gift for all the world, a means through which Jesus might manifest his glory and so bring many others to knowledge of his work in bringing salvation all the world. So, while it may seem hard to admit, the man's blindness was a wonderful gift from God. So too are many of the gifts we receive in life, which we may tend to think of as pain, suffering, or casualty. Let me give you another example.

Early one Sunday morning in Beirut in 1982, a massive invasion of the country was mounted. It rained down shrapnel all day, and bullets from automatic rifles bounced off the trees, stone walls, and houses. I was hiding in Marquand House on the side of the hill at the American University, waiting for some unknown terrorists to come and get me. I had taken out my Bible, the first one I ever had, and started to read the First Letter of John. Suddenly, the front doors crashed open, and someone came running down the center hall toward the room where I sat waiting. I was frozen in terror and couldn't move, even when the blind man Jerius Khuri stumbled into me and fell over weeping.

After some moments of recollecting myself, I realized I was in the presence of a man, even more scared than I. Imagine being blind and trapped in a city at war! He had no idea if he was running from or into danger.

In his panic he grabbed me and insisted we find the inner stone stairway, and hide under it for safety. So, quite suddenly, I was crouched in this small space under the back staircase with a shivering and weeping blind man. I was not aware that I was still holding onto my Bible, marked open to the First Letter of John.

After some brief introductions, he told me he was a translator of books for blind people of the Middle East, from Arabic, English, and French into Braille. He had been doing this for several years and had an office at the University. In turn, I told him I was a visiting professor at the medical school, and that I was scared and trying to read my newly acquired Bible. It was giving me comfort, I told him. That made Jerius angry. Really angry. He hated God, he told me. He was blind, shot between the eyes and left for dead, but instead became a blind teenager during an earlier war. They had also killed his father and tried to kill him. He could not forgive those men, nor God for his blindness and the misery he felt it brought him.

That is when it happened! I was so scared and didn't know what to do or say. So I prayed to God the prayer that has become my daily prayer. "Lord, I cannot do anything. I do not know what to say or do. Please, Lord, here are my voice and my hands and my heart. Use them to help Jerius." And, to my amazement, God said Yes, took over, and talked to Jerius. He told Jerius through my voice and heart how much He loved Jerius. He told Jerius that his blindness was a gift, not specifically for Jerius, but for all the blind people in the Middle East. With his gift of blindness, Jerius could, and did, change the lives of hundreds of blind people, trapped by their blindness in ignorance and darkness. But, because of Jerius' talent for languages and his blindness, God had chosen Jerius to bring knowledge and hope to so many with his Braille translations.

By the time we crawled out from under that staircase, Jerius was weeping tears of joy for God's love, and in thanksgiving for the gift of his blindness which allowed him to be a servant of God's kingdom. Jerius forgave himself and his fathers' killers and those who blinded them. Jerius fell in love with God that day.

That was the day that Jerius learned that his blindness was the very means by which he would come to know and love God. He could now thank God for being so gifted, for himself, for others, and for God. Jerius' blindness was a gift from God, a gift through which God could manifest love to this man who had forgotten what love and living were about. And, just like the man-born-blind in our gospel story today, Jerius did not even know that Jesus was so near to him, and so eager to give him back his spiritual sight.

I guess I was even more amazed than was Jerius. Just like a blind man myself, I did not see that God was right there, eager to help, dying to use someone's hands, mind and voice, in order to bring Jerius back into the light of Christ. I certainly did not know that God would hear my prayer and use me as his instrument of light in a deep darkness.

It was the first time I ever let God use me to help someone else. I can never forget how happy God was to have someone offer himself in service to Jerius. I did not know that I could be an instrument of helping others move from darkness into Christ's light.

Today's gospel is not only a call for all of us to shed our spiritual blindness and walk in God's light; it is also a call for each one who has received the light of Christ in Baptism to imitate Jesus in giving sight to the blind, the spiritually blind, those in darkness about the Good News of Jesus Christ. Jesus did not give this great gift of sight, as a one-time event which only he could do. Jesus performed this wonderful miracle, not just for this one man, but Jesus has done it for all who have been baptized *into Christ's light. And, his action is one which we are all to imitate - through our words and actions in this world. We are also to evangelize, and so to give sight to those in darkness.*

Soon our thoughts will be drawn to the season of Lent. Maybe this is the time for each of us in our own pilgrimage to realize that we can assist one another in making the journey to God. Let us spend some time in reflection and preparation to make Lent what it is intended to be: a new spring, a return to forgiveness, and assistance offered to others in our communal journey. And let us invite others to join us in our Lenten journey of repentance.

The purpose of Jesus' incarnation was precisely in order to take away our sins and lead us into the eternal light. We hear it repeatedly in our gospel readings. If we would be like Christ, we too have to lead others from sin and into light - in ourselves, and in others.

Indeed, we are Christ-like when we help others to seek forgiveness. Seeking forgiveness is not just a personal matter; it is a responsibility of the entire Christian community to help each other to seek and find forgiveness. Just like the blind man who needed someone to help him to recognize Christ. Just like Jerius Khuri needed someone to help him to forgive others and come into the light of Christ! Just like someone needs your help to receive God's light and life!!!

I lay down from nearly three to five when the phone rang. I could not sleep due to the electronic blaring of the Palestinian rally music and announcements next door. (Yes, it is back!) President David Dodge called to say they had not forgotten me and that no arrangement could be made. The airport will likely remain closed. The trip overland to Damascus is not safe anymore, and arrangement to get to a boat in Junieh could not be worked out. We can wait until the airport opens, possibly tomorrow, possibly next week, and meanwhile they will continue to pursue an exit by boat. I listened to BBC from five to six fifteen; we cling to all the radio reports, and ask Mohammed for translation all the time. Damour will fall tonight and the Israelis are heading inland up the mountains instead of to the south of Beirut. The dog fights and overhead artillery are no longer exciting. I am tired of it and not being able to go out due to the shrapnel.

We lost electricity during dinner and ate a lousy supper by candlelight. The food has been sparse and simple the past several days for some reason. I expect it is due partly to our acceptance of whatever is served. I've had it with a dessert of oranges and cherries on a plate, however - twice a day for most of two-and-a-half weeks is enough. And I want some percolated American coffee too!

The Palestinian radio says Yassar Arafat has called for a stop to air conflict and opening of the Beirut airport tomorrow. That has raised our hopes again. Colin has a London ticket for 12:30 and I'll get one too if the airport opens. We are on a roller coaster, one minute the possibility of departure by sea to Cyprus, then a "no" from Dodge, then an open airport possibility for tomorrow. It is silly; I'll just lay back and see for myself what happens. Colin muses about being in London tomorrow night. How nice a thought.

I want out of here!

Funny how when they called from home I couldn't know I'd be leaving, then a few hours later I knew. And I've been trying ever since to tell them, but they don't know it. I hope that they are getting my telexes. Today I was candid to them and admitted it wasn't safe here; that seemed the best thing to do. They probably know more than I do, anyway.

Wednesday, June 9, 1982

5:15 a.m.

I was awakened a while ago by the war. There is an air

attack with much ground fire here, south Beirut, I'd say. There goes our chance of the airport, I guess.

I was up most of the night with bad diarrhea. I must get something and get it quickly.

6:50 a.m.

I ran at 5:45 and returned weak and quite sick. I have no strength due to the diarrhea and it has a depleting effect. I guess I should not have run, but it is so calming to do so. But the running did not help this time.

We have no bread anymore. There is a "run" on it and we couldn't get any again today. The electronic and stereophonic Palestinian rally began about 6:30 a.m. and I am sick of it already. It is anti-American too. The bombing which started at 5:00 a.m. has not stopped yet, although it is not continuous. It appears to be south of us, about eight to ten miles, near Damour or inward from the sea.

I could not hear the war when I was in the shower.

It is later now, about seven thirty, and we are having a pause in the war sounds for nearly five minutes now. I am pleased for it. It is getting on my nerves; I know I'm safe, but I don't want to hear the sounds anymore. People are dying nearby. I guess that it is clear that I am down, stressed and tense. Maybe it is the diarrhea and weakness too.

12:40 p.m.

There is little point in writing, except to get my feelings out. The place is very tense and rumors are rampant of invasion of the city. Jets roar overhead all day now, but not much ground fire is going up at them anymore. News is hard to get as the fighting is south of the city and there is rarely electricity outside of AUB. The Israelis are supposed to invade Beirut by sea; that is the big rumor now, and fear is very great. One of the possible invasion sites is the AUB coastal beach, right in front of Marquand House. In fact, a large gun was placed there this morning after a temporary one was put there to fire at a ship and a boat. We guess that the ships are Israeli and that they have a blockade of the coast now. Having a gun so close to us is upsetting to us all here, but we cannot do anything because the narrow piece of land between the green field and sea is public highway.

Mohammed told me that Jerius got out this morning and made it to his mountain village. He was so terrified the last few days; while waiting for his ride this morning he was hit by a tiny piece of shrapnel, to top it off. He dropped to the ground and panicked. Poor man. To be blind in a war. I hope he is safe.

I went to the office for a while then came back and wrote a letter to Paul. I won't mail it here because there is no mail either. I have been napping in a chair all morning. I am not feeling too well as a result of the diarrhea. I will sleep this afternoon too, because there is nothing else to do.

2:20 p.m.

I went to check on exits. Nothing is possible, as the Israelis have us surrounded now. No ships can leave, we can't get near the airport and the overland road to Damascus has been taken. I am concerned about the fact that the Palestinians have placed their guns along the corniche, including one at AUB's green field. They are inviting an attack. I tried to call the American Embassy with no success. I am now sitting in a lady instructor's office, because she is at the American Embassy and I want to catch her when she returns. Then I may learn if they are going to help us. Perhaps they know something we don't know and are not so worried. The travel office here at AUB says a boat from Junieh is our only possible exit, if there is one at all. Of course, the airport could be allowed to open later this week, if the Palestinians don't take it over as they have threatened.

4:25 p.m.

The fighting continues all day and people are quite upset and scared as the rumors of the invasion of Beirut continue. I have been to the travel agency twice today and am happy to report results. We can go tomorrow by sea if the boats (blocking the coast) will let us pass. I leave here at 7:30 a.m. for Larnaca, Cyprus, by way of a motorcade to the east side of Beirut, and then on to Junieh.

8:17 p.m.

We are scheduled to depart AUB for Junieh tomorrow at 8:30 a.m. now, more than one hundred of us, I've heard. They are international students and four visiting professors, but it may not materialize yet. But I am ready, if a bit reserved. Once we get to Junieh, I think we will have to sit there all day and take a night boat, with the hope to be in Larnaca, after a long trip by sea, about eight o'clock or so on Friday morning. I will try to get to London then, but may have to go to Athens, they have said. We'll have to see. I am going to plan to run in the morning, possibly my last time for a day or two. But I can do it. I won't run tomorrow if it is not safe with those big guns down by the green field, especially as trigger-happy as the gunner was today!

The evening local radio said it correctly, "Terror has seized West Beirut as the Israelis approach from the south side with a hundred tanks and troops and we are surrounded by destroyers, and overhead are the bombs." I am personally scared. Having the diarrhea may be as much related to that as the lack of proper food and water these recent days. The war has suddenly moved from being radio reports and sounds, to being scenes. The five Israeli war ships that we can see as we look out our front door and down across the green field are terrible to consider. One shot at the gunner by the green field, but it fell short. Everybody just watched to see how close the ship could come, that is, the shell shot from the destroyer. The rumors are that we will have a night of bombing and an attack on West Beirut in the morning. I hope not, as I want out of here, and I don't want all the hand-to-hand fighting and bloodshed here.

Everybody is so scared; the poor students just stand around as the guns on the corniche and all around us blaze at the overhead bombers. It is beyond most emotion to express what I feel and what others are feeling. I am so sorry that I'm putting my family and friends through this; I cannot imagine what they think as they hear the reports of the war and its effects on us here in Beirut.

I walked over and said good-by to Nabil Kronfol. He is a pathetic and sad man now. I saw his wife and hardly recognized her. She was gray and sad in the face. They can't get away like maybe I can. They are angry at America too, as so many here seem to be, because America is not doing anything to stop this. All those Israeli guns and bombs and planes are American made and given, they say. They (We) could be killed by American-made instruments of war. The destruction and bloodshed that are being reported is terrible here. We don't have any TVs or newspapers to see and learn like you do in America now. We just rely on the several radio stations, and we are totally addicted to the radios and rumor mills.

Our Embassy cannot and will not help, we learned, and our policies do not allow them to give us advice or direction. We Americans, are quite simply, expendable commodities of the current American policies at this time.

Chuck Breindel and Nabil Kronfol at the office in happier times.

Each night as I go to bed I read a prayer of Francis de Sales. It goes like this: "Do not look forward to what might happen tomorrow; the same everlasting Father who cares for you today, will care for you tomorrow and every day. Either He will shield you from suffering or He will give you unfailing strength to bear it. Be at peace, then, and put aside all anxious thoughts and imaginings."

Thursday, June 10, 1982

4:45 a.m.

The shooting of the big guns down in front of us began about four this morning and so ended my sleep. There have been jets overhead ever since. I did my bathroom business, I prayed we would get out today, and I am getting my hopes up. I will run and then be ready to go.

6:25 a.m.

I came down at five and found everybody, including Colin, on the porch. The war had started and it was heated. I was told not to go down to the green field because there were Palestinians down there with guns - inside AUB campus walls! I could not believe it. I was very frightened. (A group of soldiers with machine guns has just passed by Marquand House.) I ran over to the Medical Entrance gate and I passed a Palestinian with a machine gun on his back, half way there. I nodded to him but I did not speak for fear that he would recognize me as American. The air attack continued and has not yet stopped. It is quite horrible.

I went over to the oval and ran some laps about it, and all the while the guns. Guns, guns, guns. I don't think I feel anything anymore. I don't even hide when the shrapnel is falling.

I nearly cried while showering, due to the tension and my concern for safety. When you awaken in Virginia about seven hours from now, I can imagine what you will hear about the approaching war in Beirut and possibly on AUB's lovely campus. I hope that you remember those words you wrote to me in my card. I hope we get out of here today. I learned that the AUB telex is broken down, so that you will not be getting my cable. I guess it is just as well.

Later, at breakfast - Manakeesh and coffee.

I hope we get out of here. Colin is a bit pessimistic, but I am not. I can't wait to see everyone back at home. After I am home and comfortable, I want to talk to Hayes and Paul and the rest of the guys about my experiences here and about some of my feelings, and get their reactions. I need to get all of this out of me. I've got it all bottled up in me and I can't afford to acknowledge my feelings or let them out, at least, not yet.

Today is the beginning of a Curcillo weekend for the ladies back home. I had thought I might be there for it. At least I was thinking that earlier this week. Now I hope I am home for the last day of it, on Sunday. I will keep them all in my prayers and thoughts throughout this weekend, despite my other compelling thoughts.

7:10 a.m.

There is shooting on campus - shooting at the acting president's home, a short distance from here. The bullets are bouncing off the trees near here. There is gunfire everywhere and I am scared.

7:30 a.m.

There are bullets flying all around campus. There must be some crazies out there somewhere. It appears that they are not firing at the acting president's home, as was being said, but at anything. I have to pack my diary now, and get ready to go. God bless us and guide us in safety today.

I left a letter for Jerius if he ever comes back and I have letters for Mohammed and Hassan with money in them. They are so dear, and I am so grateful for them.

The Main Gate of AUB, what I hoped would be my final sight of the University.

11:55 a.m.

We waited at some Dean's office with the about one hundred international students until 1:00 in order to leave, and finally we got in some trucks (like cattle trucks), but they put us four visiting professors in a car between the two trucks of students. And we got ready to go out through the main gate of AUB and into the streets. The buses that were supposed to take us never showed up due to the intensity of the war, we were told. It was a very tense time, considering how dangerous it has become. When we all got to the gate to leave the campus, we were stopped by a cavalcade of maybe two hundred students. Then out on the street there was a radical group of young people, many with guns, who were looking for Americans. They spotted us because we were in a car instead of packed in the trucks. They told us to get out of the car. My driver literally threw me out of the car, along with Bob Norton, the other visiting professor from Utah. That was about fifteen minutes ago.

I was so terrified and we thought they would kill us, but they did not point any weapons at us as we stood against the wall with our backs to them. We expected a firing-squad mentality. When nothing happened, Bob and I ran back into the AUB gate. I called the president's office while standing at the gate and that is where we are sitting now, in his office. Those moments along the wall with all the angry students and the presence of guns - I could hardly stand up; my legs would not support me as I stood there. We are still so frightened and unsure.

The president says they will try to find a way to get us out, me and Bob Norton, whom I just met. Now that they know we are here, and what we look like, we are in great danger, we have learned. I'm trying to be calm, but cannot. I've never been so afraid before in my whole life. I must pray. What an experience after so long a delay for two days and then the wait all morning. How could they take us out of the cavalcade to freedom? I must pray and trust.

Do you know how I felt when they grabbed me? I was afraid they were going to kill me, and I hoped that if that was going to happen, that they would give me a chance to tell them who I was, my children's names, where I was from, and why I was here, so that I would not have to die unknown. I did not want to be killed by them because I represented something they hated. If I were to die, I wanted them to know exactly whom they were killing, and that I was a person and not a "cause." Isn't that strange?

[Note: On the first anniversary of 9/11, I preached about the incident above, as follows below.]

Before the Firing Squad

September 11, 2002 (Wednesday of the 23rd week, II): Luke 6:20-26

When Jesus talked to those who were suffering, hungry, poor, and weeping, he recognized their experiences of sadness and anguish. But Jesus did not dwell on the past. Jesus pointed them toward the future. Listen again to the phrases of Jesus to them: ... you will be satisfied. ... you will laugh. ... your reward will be great in heaven. (Luke 6:21, 23)

Jesus' entire ministry was about healing, about moving forward on a journey of life, into and through pain and difficulty, with a sure and certain knowledge that God's loving plan would heal us and offer us joy and peace. Jesus is for us "the light of the world." Jesus brings light into darkness. But how do we move forward into the future to be light for the world?

One year ago today the world experienced one of the worst acts of hatred, one that was not even imaginable. How do we make sense out of such hatred? How can we grow after we recognize the power of hatred in the world? Why and how could someone hate so much at that?

Let me tell you about an experience I had twenty years ago this summer that shed light for me on the cause of hatred and the way to overcome it. Along with two friends Bob and Colin, I was captured by some terrorists in the Middle East. We were pulled from our car, and made to stand against a stone wall, with our backs to the men with machine guns. The plan appeared to kill us by firing squad. Until September 11 of last year [2001], that was the most terrifying moment of my life. After some unknown period of time, they did not shoot us so we started to run down the street. We figured that we'd rather be shot in the back running away, than standing still. But they did not shoot, and we got away. When I sat down later that day, I was amazed that those men wanted to kill us; they did not even know who we were. I prayed and reflected on how someone could hate so much. And I came to this insight: Those men did not hate ME; they did not even know my name. What they hated was something that I represented to them. I did not know what that was, and it might have been something that did not even apply to me. They had assigned some label to me, a label that stood for something they hated. It was the label that they wanted to kill, and not me.

That is the key to understanding hatred. People don't hate people; they hate labels they assign to people. The ability to hate is based largely on being able to stereotype people, by giving them a label. We have all heard of hatred: hatred of foreigners, of Mexicans, of Americans, of Catholics, of Jews, of conservatives or liberals, ... - whatever. If you want to hate someone you don't know, give them a label and hate the label.

That is what happened last year on September 11th. The people who attacked America did not hate those who died or were injured; their hatred was for something that existed in their imaginations, some label or stereotype they created. And it took them years to learn to develop that label, and to learn to hate it. That is how hatred happens.

But hatred is not natural. People have to learn to hate. That is why Jesus often used a child as an example of someone who could enter the kingdom of heaven. Children do not know how to hate, but only to love and trust. They have to be taught to hate.

So, how can we overcome the remembrance of this hatred? We who have the light of Christ in us, can let it shine out into a world of darkness and hatred. We can refuse to hate, by refusing to label people. We can recognize every person as an individual, not a label, knowing full well that God loves everyone of us. And, refusing to label people, we can then see in others the same kind of goodness that has been so apparent in our country after September 11th, as countless men and women reached out to strangers to offer love, blood, sweat, money and so much more.

The world will not be conquered by hatred; the world will not be conquered by violence. The world will be conquered by God who is love. The source of this love can only be those who have the light of Christ in them. The instruments of making a brighter future are here tonight, in this church. Just as Jesus healed while on this earth, so now we, the parts of the body of Christ, must carry on the ministry of healing.

The only way that we can counter these random acts of terrorism, the only way that we can counter these random acts of violence, is with random acts of kindness, and random acts of love. We must be as indiscriminate and aggressive in doing good, in showing kindness, as those who spread evil or violence.

That is what we have to do - let the light of Christ shine out of us to anyone we meet, in any situation where love or kindness is needed, at any time we may encounter the opportunity to show love or kindness. If you want to conquer the world through Christ, resolve this evening to be a committer of random acts of kindness. As you move through the day, wherever you are, with whoever you are, whenever, if you see the opportunity to do something kind, just do it. Like the old song says: "If everyone lit just one little candle, what a bright world this would be."

Let us affirm our faith in the principles of freedom of our country and the underlying values of the Good News of Jesus Christ that enables us to say: IN GOD, WE TRUST.

As a sign of our solidarity with those who have died, as a sign of our commitment to create a better world, infused with the light of Christ, I invite you to come forward and light a candle, and then place it in the vases of sand.

3:40 p.m.

Another three and a half hours had gone by as we sat in a panic. We left the President's office once to go with a special driver named Omar. After waiting in a garage for about fifteen minutes, we were taken back to the President's office for more pow-wows among them about us. I was so frightened because there was an air raid, discussions of another Iran-hostage situation but now at AUB with us. Finally more discussions with the students at the gate, and we left again with Omar, got into the car, both on the floor of the back seat so we would not be seen. Omar waited for bombing and a rain of shrapnel so that the streets would be empty of people. There was a high speed run to get us to the border (the green line where the city is demarcated as East and West). We were dropped out in front of the museum at the entrance to East Beirut. Just then another car containing two AUB medical graduate students pulled up and we were told to jump in the back to be brought to Junieh after we would go through a few checkpoints and inspections. We caught up with the AUB crowd of international students soon because the Israelis had blocked the port and taken them all. We were taken at gun-point to join them. We are all now sitting in an apartment lobby outside of Junieh where we will be staying indefinitely. There are no rooms for any of us to have any privacy. We were thinking that they might let us four professors have a room somewhere. (We have been joined by Colin who was in one of the trucks and by an Indian professor named Prakesh Gupta).

There are guards with machine guns around the doors. There are about a hundred people being held in this one room, and there is a stairwell down two floors to a single bathroom. There is a "store" of sorts with a bit of food still there. The students have gotten the food. I don't know where we will sleep, what we will eat, or what we will do. Many of the students are Muslim, and it is not safe for them to be here in East Beirut, and they are quite terrified. Talk of death churns the rumor mill.

What is going on in Beirut? Terror reigns there: no communications, no electricity, Israeli gunboats offshore, soldiers and radical militia roaming all over. The campus is unsafe for the first time ever, as bullets whiz by, and groups of soldiers/militia roam about. The tears of tension and fear will never come to me, as my emotions are beyond such expression now. I think I am safe here, and I will be happy to sit on the floor of a cargo ship to Larnaca whenever one is allowed in to take us. Meanwhile, I thank God for sparing me again; I think we are the last from AUB to make it out.

The Israelis dropped yellow leaflets all over the city about ten o'clock this morning. They told the Syrian troops to get out and offered them three hours and two alternate routes for departing. Then the Israelis said they would attack the city, even kill the Syrian army that remained. So we are just in time and quite lucky.

Waiting for all those hours this morning for the cattle trucks to haul us out, a student rolled up a newspaper and pretended it was a gun, called me American, and shot me. Another fellow handed me a leftist newspaper in Arabic; it had pictures of the devastation. He said I must show it to the Americans when I got home so they could see the truth, rather than the trash in our papers. (I am sure he is right too, about what is in our newspapers back home.) He scared me very badly.

Riding here I sang to myself, as best I could the first line of that song "Be Not Afraid, I Go Before You Always," We have a long hard time ahead of us and don't know when or where we will get anywhere. Maybe there will be a cease fire. Maybe the embassies and AUB can negotiate our safe departure.

I want to remember and thank, at least in my prayers, all the people who got me out today: Samia Jordak, Omar Faour, David Dodge, Dr. Georges Freyha and others that I don't know. (There was a Sudanese student H. Bashir, and he gave me a sandwich, juice and water when I got out of the car in Junieh by the harbor; he was so dear, and to me, a sympathetic model of brotherhood. I wonder if he had food enough for himself.)

Later ...

I don't think it is good for a man to fear for his life. Today I learned how badly I want to live and how afraid I am of death - no, not death, but violent death. I am afraid I'm going to be in sad shape when I return home too, and maybe I won't know how to cope. But, for now, I must, until I get home to safety.

8:40 p.m.

We are in a small room off the lobby where the rest are being kept. The four of us professors have been given a room for the night and don't have to sleep on the floor of the other room with all the international students. There are actually two small beds in the room. We will be kept here overnight, we understand. As the Israelis would not let us out, who knows when we will be out, but we will try again tomorrow evening to get off by a boat, I have heard. Whatever else this gift of a room signifies, it means that our captors, well-armed as they are, don't seem to intend the four of us any harm. I hope that is what it means anyway.

There are two teachers upstairs, one of them from the AUB east campus and another, a high school principal. They are Maronite Christians we learned, much to our amazement. They sent their sons down to the lobby and they discretely found me about 5:30 p.m. and they invited me to follow them up the stairs. I was scared because I did not know who they were or what they wanted. I did not know if they were going to help or harm me. But I followed them when no one was looking. They let me bring one of the other professors too, and they fed us bread and cheese and cake and ham too. We were treated so wonderfully by these four people who didn't even know us, and who have very little to eat themselves. After all these scary days, it was like angels from heaven. They helped us just because they were once refugees, like us, running from war. When they saw the trucks of people arrive, they came to see if they could help someone. They felt bad that they could not help all of us, and I felt guilty that they were treating us to something to eat when all of the students were huddled downstairs so frightened. I'll tell you about the amazing visit with them later.

The Israelis let the Cypriot students among us go, but no one else could get a boat today. So here we are, mostly students, on a floor in the back of the apartment/hotel. We will try to negotiate to go tomorrow evening, I heard again. I will try to find a way to cable you all on Saturday. I guess I will miss the Curcillo closing on Sunday.

AUB was bombed today after we left, on the green field. We heard it on a small radio that a student has. West Beirut is at war, and we got out! So many did not.

The two ladies and their two sons and Professor Gupta and I went together and prayed tonight for five minutes. It was their idea and I was pleased. I trust God tonight. I'll accept my time here, my cargo boat ride to Cyprus, the dirt and poor conditions. But I'll never forget the horror of war, the terror of being a war refugee, or the spontaneous goodness of good people. Good night!

[Note to the readers: I wrote about the incident above in my earlier book, in the story of Michel below.]

Michel

3rd Sunday, A: Exodus 17:3-7, John 4:5-42

Sometimes we just have to take a risk, and go forward based on faith alone. Just like the Samaritan woman at the well did when she spoke to Jesus, when she went to the village and told the others, when they came and heard Jesus and believed in Him. Sometimes we just have to take a risk, like she did. I've had to take the risk of faith too.

During my time of captivity in Beirut, I had dysentery and diarrhea as did the others. Sometimes I was so thirsty and hungry that it was hard to think clearly. From the others who were with me (and understood Arabic much better than I did), I learned that we were being held prisoners on the ground floor of an apartment building in Junieh, and that there may be people on the floors above us. I did not know if the people up there were our captors, or their families, or perhaps people trapped by the war and as hungry and thirsty as I was. I did not know if they were friendly or hostile, but I was willing to take the risk to find out. I was so thirsty and hungry.

On the second evening there, there were no soldiers in sight when a 16-year old boy named Michel stuck his head into the room where I was being held. It was a stairway door, apparently unguarded, unless perhaps this boy was one of them. He motioned to me to come. I did not know what to do, but he beckoned again. So I took the risk and put my faith in this olive-skinned stranger. If I was being taken away to be killed, I did not know. But I decided to trust. Like the Samaritan woman at the well did when she encountered Jesus.

We ascended the stairway to the third or fourth floor and entered a small apartment. There was Michel's mother Latiffe and another woman and her teenaged son, all sitting on the floor around a small table covered by greasy wrapping paper and bottles. I was scared that they were the families of the soldiers and that I was being set up. But once again, I had to decide to run, or to listen. I took the risk and listened -- like the woman did at the well. What followed was an encounter with Christ, a most amazing gift in my life.

The women were widowed, they told me; their husbands were already killed. They were trapped above us in what was supposed to be an abandoned apartment. They had little food, but the boys knew when the guards changed, and how and where to sneak out for food. So they were surviving for the time being. They had learned who we were -- the political captives from the American University of Beirut on the first floor. They had little to eat, but they wanted to share some of it with me. On the table were a block of white goat cheese, some pita bread, some very bruised fruit, and bottles of water. They said: "Eat and drink. We want to help you live." But I was scared and doubtful. It was too good to be true. Just like the Samaritan woman at the well; Jesus' words were too good to be true. Just like her, it seemed too much to believe.

Then this young boy, who had come for me, said the most amazing thing I ever heard from a teenager. He said: "I came for you. It is what Jesus would do." They were Christians, I learned. And I began to cry! He took off a cross and chain from around his neck, hung it on the back of an upholstered chair, like a makeshift altar, and asked me to pray with them. I tried to, but could only listen. When I got composed, I told them that I couldn't eat when my colleagues downstairs were so hungry and thirsty too. I wanted to go and get them.

But the two mothers were concerned. They did not have enough food and water to share with all of us. It might cause them to go hungry and thirsty. I was embarrassed and wanted only to share my portion. The boys, all smiles and confidence, led me down another stairwell and back into the prisoner room on the first floor. With deft skill, we avoided the guards, and the boys brought all three of us back to the apartment. We ate and drank, and prayed together before the makeshift altar. As we ate, the life-giving food seemed to multiply itself. We left quickly, taking some additional food inside our shirts and we returned to captivity. I did not care if we were missed by the guards, or even if we were caught. We had met Jesus. He had given us life-giving food and water. He had taken care of us, and I knew he would continue to do so, no matter what.

It took a leap of faith, a risk, to believe the words of an olive-skinned young man. But it led to an encounter with Christ. Ever since that day so many years ago, I am constantly attentive to hear Jesus' Word in my environment. I do not ever want to miss a chance to experience his life-giving faith.

Like the Samaritan woman at the well, sometimes you just have to take a risk, have faith in the Word you hear, and go forward into the unknown in order to meet Christ. I pray that you hear his Word today and respond in faith.

The next time you see a stranger, perhaps someone whom you would never want to spend any time with, take a second look, listen, and be prepared for the possibility of finding Christ in the words you hear. Or better yet, the next time you encounter a stranger, perhaps you can be the Christ-presence to him or her, through your words and your deeds.

May you be constantly nourished by the Word of the Sacred Scriptures so that you may be prepared for your encounter at the well of life-giving water. May the waters of Baptism which flowed over you, now flow through you, and out to others who seek to receive that same life-giving water.

Friday, June 11, 1982
At the "Holiday Beach" in Junieh, Lebanon [I learned the name of this place.]

6:20 a.m.

I slept on the mattress with Bob who snores a lot. It was a restless night but seemed luxurious because we were not on the cement floor of the lobby room with all the students. I went out on the back street for a bit, early this morning, and that was just wonderful. No one saw me; I could have gotten away. But where would I go; I feel safer being held here by gunmen than by being out there in a war zone. I had been told not to go out when I tried, but I could not help it. No one was looking. I had been awake for about forty-five minutes before that and used a towel that Prakesh had, and then rinsed my underwear to hang outside on the railing. I put my dirty clothes back on, as who knows how long it will be before we will be able to get clean clothes. We are hopeful of leaving late today, by a cargo boat. But we will be patient. [We live on rumors, and survive based on hopeful ones.] It is hell in Beirut, and I'll always remember President Dodge's efforts to get me out of AUB and Beirut these past days. The city is controlled by gunmen, militia, anyone with a gun and, at the same time, it is being attacked and bombed by the Israelis.

9:10 a.m.

I went downstairs and talked to the students a while and sat with the Sudanese group. I offered our room for use to two ladies with a three-month-old baby in their care. They washed, did some baby laundry, etc. Meanwhile, I went up to the room of Mrs. Latifee Asmer and her 16-year-old son Michel who came to give me some breakfast. They were so kind again, and fed me toast, cheese, butter and jam, in addition to some coffee. Her son wants to come to the United States, to George Washington University next year and so they were eager for advice from an American professor like me too.

There was word of a navy rescue today and hopes are high. But it is nothing but a wished-for rumor. No news at all so far today; the rumor is that we will hear something about 1:00 p.m. about how we can get a cargo boat to take us out of here.

This is like a dream. I can't believe that this is happening to me. One of the students said she thought she was watching a lousy movie in which she was an actress, and that it was just a fictional story and not real. No one ever thought it would become dangerous, that AUB would not be a safe place. Whatever else has happened in Beirut, AUB has always been a neutral and safe haven in difficult times.

There are Palestinian students from Jordan here among us. They are terrified, really fearful for their lives. They believed they were going to be killed when they came here to the East side of Beirut; they came because they were equally afraid to stay at AUB, they said. You would not believe what they thought would happen if they came here. (Some here do hate them too, and won't speak to them in the lobby where we are being held.)

I hope that all are asleep back home. I still have not been able to get through to them. Please be at peace.

10:55 p.m.

I'm exhausted but o.k. Having a hard time relaxing and hanging on. Tense, nervous, and worried about you all back home. Maybe one of my cables got through, though. Maybe you got to the State Department and they know where I am. I guess you must assume that I am safe at AUB. I suppose I will get home and find you nonchalant about all this, never worried or upset, never knowing about this situation. I hope so; it comforts me to think so anyway. Ignorance is bliss, if you can do it.

We have three small and slow cargo boats waiting to take us out of here later this afternoon, we've learned. And we finally contacted the American Embassy to try to negotiate our departure. These are the latest rumors. We are hopeful. We have been without our passports since we were taken here. They were taken by our captors, who we are told are the Ktieb, the Christian Phalangist militia.

2:05 p.m.

The cease fire is real and has now lasted two hours. The massive bombings which were so intense late this morning have stopped. Maybe we will get out of here today.

I cannot believe all that happened to me yesterday. It was a miracle that we got out and could only be the result of prayers.

I have lain down for forty-five minutes and have taken some of the medicine that Dr. Georges Freyha got me. It is for gastrointestinal infection and I am sure that it will work. That will relieve one problem of the cargo boat crossing, which may occur tonight. I'll go see what is up now.

4:30 p.m.

It appears that we will not be going anywhere. The Israelis have sorted through our passports and have approved all but two or three of us to go, we hear, but it is not final yet. So we'll see what is next.

A lady from AUB administration came and told us about AUB. It was occupied by the Palestinians and still is. The green field was not bombed, but the Engineering Building was occupied and bombed. The faculty are in shelters or are barricaded in their homes. The situation is horrible as armed gunmen roam about everywhere on the campus.

9:30 p.m.

We are still at the Holiday Beach and Michel has offered two of us to come upstairs and sleep in his room. Prakesh and I have accepted; Bob and Colin will sleep on the floor with the students, because we gave our little room to the Sudanese mother and baby. They need it much more than we do. We are so tired, but at peace somewhat. Some students are distressed.

I learned that negotiations continue, and we could even leave during the night, but that is not logical. We may find that tomorrow afternoon is more feasible; who knows how long we will be held here?

We organized a student sing-along out on the patio of the lobby room tonight for one and a half hours, and that was a very good idea. Even a guitar appeared from somewhere and we had fun and laughed together. It relieved some tension, and the captors just watched. I was pleased to be able to help organize it.

Saturday, June 12, 1982

9:30 a.m.

We are all in a good mood after a good night's sleep. Some students had mats to sleep on and they slept well too. There were several meetings after I went to sleep. Colin attended for us. The clearances have been received and we have only to get confirmation from the captain of the blockade ship. We expect it this morning and will likely leave today. Spirits are high; I hope they are not too high.

Colin awakened us at 5:30 a.m. with the news. I went with

Michel out of the building again, and then had some coffee with him and his mother. Now I am trying to contact the family. I am going to try to telex Colin's girlfriend in London and have her contact home, if possible. I hope Colin can get a telex and that he can add my request. I don't know how or who is involved in this effort. But, if it happens, I will be able to relax a bit, no matter what else. My family is my main worry now.

My diarrhea remains, but it is better. I think the pills helped. I have some water and a banana and a piece of cheese for the trip on the sea. I got them at the little store. We will be on the deck of a big flat cargo ship for 14 to 16 hours, they told us. There is no water or food, and it will be very cold, especially at night. I am going to organize some games and singing for the ship, like last night. It went so well then. Normally, if I felt like I feel now, with headache and diarrhea and exhaustion, I would be sick. But it is relative, and I have not felt so good in days! I sang our national anthem as I walked today.

10:45 a.m.

I could not get through to London on the telex. But I found a man from Abu Dhabi who offered to have his office there call you if we can get a telex to there. I am trying, but all the lines are gone now. I'd rather use Abu Dhabi because it is Muslim, and they work on Saturdays and Sundays. (Their Sabbath is Friday.) So it will get through and you may know of my safety right away. Won't you be surprised if someone from Abu Dhabi calls the house about me? (I wonder if my telex from Tuesday got through, or the one I planned to send on Wednesday. Surely the AUB telex worked sometime.)

The bombing in Beirut is bad again today. It shook the place about midnight and again about six a.m. here. I hope it is not bad. Selfishly, I hope it does not screw up our great escape.

2:25 p.m., and on our way at last!

We left the apartment/hotel by car, five of us and got here to the pier at 12:45 p.m. Finally, the first bus load arrived, and there are two more buses to come. There is a calm sea, but very hot and humid here at the port. I will fry in the sun and burn in the wind, but I am ready for the long ride. We had planned to leave by three, but it will be closer to five, I expect. The flat cargo boat is called the S.S. Edy, and it lays ahead of us in the harbor, an unimpressive thing, a flat metal barge with a small "house" near the rear. That is all there is.

Spirits are high among us. We have been told to be prepared for an interception by the Israeli blockade ships. We have got our speaker chosen, a Lebanese-American first-year medical student. He is the only one who will speak for us, no matter what. That is important if we should be stopped and boarded. Only he will speak, and we will be calm and confident, no matter what. That is what we have agreed to.

I hope that we are going, but I am still cautious.

If all goes completely smooth, I will be home on Monday night; that is, if we leave this afternoon and if we can get connections and leave Cyprus tomorrow. I'll not have much confidence in that; it is not good to do so, I think.

4:30 p.m.

I am now sitting on a tug boat and waiting to be taken to the cargo ship S.S. Edy. It is probably about ninety degrees in the sun and there is a clear sky. I wish I'd have thought of a hat. We are all so tired and hot, but excited. Most of us have a little bit of food and/or water. I found a part of a cardboard box on the pier and have that with me. I can use it to cover myself from the sun, I think.

5:15 p.m.

All appear to be on board the S.S. Edy. Boy, it is crude! All of our luggage and about 100+ people, I would guess, are on the filthy metal top of this cargo ship (They call it a "barge.") There is a tarpaulin stretched over the front part of it and some students have brought their things and are sitting on them and some are even sleeping. It is horribly crowded. We will have a terrible trip, but we won't notice it, I hope, at least not too much. It is fitting that my shirt is already ruined; all my clothes will be done in by tomorrow, but I'll fly if I can, no matter what is my condition, and no matter what I have to wear.

The people on the Edy as I could count them, by country

Senegal	1	Abu Dhabi	1
Nepal	2	United Arab Emirates	1
Maldives	27	Kuwait	2
India	1	Bahrain	3-5
Bangladesh	3	Qatar	2-3
Australian	1	Egypt	
Jordan	46, I think.	Somalia	2
Lebanon	1	Djibouti	2-3
Ethiopia	1	England	2
Sudan	4-5	Spain	1
Saudi Arabia	2	USA	11

22 countries

[The above list was on a small yellow piece of lined paper that I found in my diary. I don't know when it was written.]

7:06 p.m. on the Mediterranean Sea, off the coast of Junieh,
Lebanon

We set out about 6:30 p.m., but I cannot sit until we pass
the Israeli navy boat. It is about a half to three-quarters of a
mile off the port now. I do not think they are approaching us
now. I think we are free. We just have to last for another few
days. I'm having trouble hanging on now. The relief, the
down, the fear to believe we are going to get away!

There has been heavy bombing in Beirut since we left and
the sounds travel very well across the water. Our farewell
travesty!

9:30 p.m.

The Israeli ship stopped us at about eight o'clock and ran
search lights over us. We all had to stand up straight on the
deck, with our hands over our heads. After lots of talk and
tension here, we were allowed to go on again.

Sunday, June 13, 1982

12:35 a.m.

We went for about a half hour before the Israeli ship
stopped us again. They demanded to take the Captain and
our student leader Paul. That was nearly three hours ago and
we have not moved. People here are tense, perhaps frightened. I don't know. No one dares speak to anyone else. We
all expect to be boarded, searched, and who knows what else.

They have just told us all to rise and stand on board in
sight. (I have not.) They are passing over us with a huge
bright beam of light as we line the barge, hands up high.
Personally, I think we have been cleared and they are just
taunting us, because of their captain's arrogance and pride. I
am tense, but not afraid for my safety. This must be what they

call psychological warfare. Even if we sail right now, we will not make Larnaca before the end of tomorrow afternoon. Does this mean another day's delay?

5:10 a.m.

Later they came back and took three more students for a total of four. I was so proud of those three students who courageously crawled over the side of this barge into the waiting arms of those pontoon boats loaded for bear with artillery. They called out names across the sea, tossed ropes, and demanded the ones called to come over the side to the pontoon boats, with the red-eyed bazookas pointed at them.

Then they told the rest of us to lie down on the surface of the barge and go to sleep. We obeyed and the barge started up again. We awakened with the sun, a short while ago and listened to the bombing of Lebanon. It was very severe during the night. It was horrible to be at sea and watching Beirut being bombed, as we were being terrorized by the Israelis from their submarine. (Or is it submarines?)

We are now slowly moving south down the coast of Lebanon about ten miles out from the shore. We are not going to Larnaca! Nearly twelve hours and we are still nowhere. We don't know what they will do next. I am wondering if anybody knows where we are - like our embassies! We have been taken captive by the Israeli navy and I don't think anyone knows it.

7:40 a.m.

Everyone is up now, the heat is great and people are mostly lying around, resting with their faces covered for protection from the elements. We are filthy with dirt and grease and sweat; I expect we will all throw our clothes away when we have something else to wear. I continue to remain under the

tarpaulin and the cardboard box, protected as I can be. I lay
on top of the piece of cardboard box for comfort during the
short night.

Some students have asked the captain if we are going anywhere. His instructions, he said, are to go to the port of Haifa,
Israel, very slowly, about five knots per hour (whatever that
means). We should be there about eleven tonight perhaps.

How do people feel here? Tired, exhausted, tense, afraid,
frustrated, mostly. We have not done anything and we have
been taunted, victimized and harassed at every possible occasion.
For myself, I found tears in my eyes earlier, but I would not give
in; I don't know what else I have to endure yet.

The sea is still calm and the night was not too cold, and we
are away from the war. They say there is a cease fire again.
Last night we watched the huge bombs and explosions about
Beirut during that final horrible fighting before the assumed
cease fire. We were all terrified by the magnitude of the
bombs and the fire and the glow of the skies.

There are many theories floating around this boat as to
why we are being taken to Haifa (if indeed we are going there).
One is that they want to take us as hostages, another is that
they want to seize and search us. Another is that they want to
parade their warfare to us and search us. But here is my
favorite theory among the people on the barge. They are going
to make propaganda and "save us." They will take us in and
help us get home. Some say that they will fly us to Larnaca or
elsewhere, or that we will be bussed to Tel Aviv to the airport.
I even dreamed that the U.S. would fly me home or fly you to
me. (I wish someone knew where I was, and that I am o.k.)

I must say, the Christian phalangists (Ktieb) were good to
us during the time they held us captive in Junieh, and Dr.
Freyha and Professor Abdullah Sfier were so helpful. We
learned that the militia who held us had not slept in five days.

9:05 a.m.

The Israelis have returned and they brought back the four students they took during the night at sea. Now they say they will board us, and they are demanding all our cameras, film, etc. - anything that could create a record of the recent days. Then they are going to search us. I will hide this diary and dare them to find it. We will never reach Larnaca if we don't surrender all our things, they just said. They intend to board and search us and maybe bomb us if we don't comply with all of their demands.

1:25 p.m.

We are all exhausted, but still continue south along the coast at a very slow pace. We are about out of any food and water too. People are listless and just sit and lie about.

For myself, I am ill and headache is very intense. The diarrhea has not abated. I try to lie still on a piece of cardboard I got at the Junieh pier, and try to cover myself from the sun. We are tense, and don't know where we are going or why. Some say we are going past Haifa port and will be headed for a port called Jaffa. I tried to pray but can't think clearly now. I recalled that all at home were at morning prayers an hour ago, as that moment went by here. So was I, in spirit.

We Americans want to request that the Israelis give our names to the embassy so that they can inform our families that we are here and alive. It is a good idea if we can do it - if they will let us do it. (If we do have to spend another whole day on this hot, stinky deck, we'll have lots of physical and psychological illnesses. We started this trip at noon yesterday from the Holiday Beach, twenty-five and a half hours ago, and after two-and-a-half days of exhaustion and fear.)

3:00 p.m.

We are in Haifa harbor and another Israeli ship has approached. They have boarded us again with their machine guns (American made and given!). I guess we'll be searched again now. There are several sick people, but even they have sat up for this. I see nine or ten on the aft deck area below the captain's place. They all look like teenagers with machine guns.

They are putting us into groups according to our nationality and have begun to question us a while ago. When my nationality was identified as American, they were brief with me. The large group of Jordanian students were grouped together and given a pretty good talking to; I think Israelis don't like Jordanian people.

6:30 p.m.

We were checked out by the Israelis. They went all through the boat, checked our passports, then they fed us. They brought on board crates of cucumbers, oranges, tomatoes, cheese, yogurt, bread, olives, halvah, water and juice, and we ate and ate. Hard to see with our eyes full of tears, by the way. We feel good for the first time in a long, long time. No one is trying to hurt us, no bombs are falling, and I don't think anyone is any longer afraid of their machine guns or threats.

Now they say that the American counsel wants to see the passports of all the Americans on board. So they've come and taken them from us and we wait. They promised to contact our families for us too. (I have become the unofficial spokesman since Paul seems to have had a mental breakdown from his nighttime treatment when they took him overboard and away.) I bitched about the lack of assistance from the Beirut office of the American consulate in front of the Israelis, and that was stupid of me. One of the others quickly told me to be quiet; I was so sorry I did that.

I feel full of decent food finally. It has been over a week since I had enough food. I also asked to use the toilet on the barge, and I had a chance to wash my face for the first time. I would like to go again but there is no chance of that. I have pushed as far as I could. I am hoping that the American Counsel will let us come to shore and help us to get home soon. I dread the thoughts of another day or two on this tugboat. We are all so excited now to know that someone on shore knows that we are out here and being held by the Israelis.

Even if I can get to shore, most of the others on this boat cannot, because they are from nations that do not recognize Israel. For those students, this escapade in Haifa harbor is particularly terrifying, as the murmuring along the deck makes all too clear. I have talked to several of the young soldiers who are holding us now, and I have reminded them that their guns, uniforms and boots were paid for by me. They were all a bit embarrassed and sheepish about holding us Americans at gun-point, but they said they were doing their duty. One of the fellows said he had been in Sidon just a day or two ago, that he was getting out of the military in two months and that he could not wait. Another told me that Friday was his last day of service and he was so happy. He was planning to come to the United States to study, on scholarship, I assume.

This whole experience has been a total nightmare. I am no longer hopeful of anything, nor surprised by anything. I have had it, but during these three to four hours of Israeli search, I have gotten a grasp on myself. Maybe because I know that my family will soon know where I am. It has been most painful to be "lost" to the world these days.

Monday, June 14, 1982

2:40 a.m., in Tel Aviv

After hours of waiting, we were told at ten p.m. that the American Counsel, a Mr. Brown, wanted to see us on shore and that we Americans could take our bags and stay there if we wanted to. The Counsel wanted to match all the passports he had seen with a live body, it was reported, and he was not willing to come board to do so, but wanted the Israelis to produce a living human being from among those on the ship as a match for every American passport.

I could not bear another twenty-four hours lying on the deck of the S.S. Edy, so I left willingly. A tug boat came out to the barge. I shouted out to it when I learned the American Counsel was aboard, nearly got shot for that, but no longer cared, and was taken on board the tug. All eleven Americans were taken ashore on a little tugboat, then treated to some questions by the Israelis in a warehouse, and released. There were discussions between the Counsel and some Israeli honcho. There were Mr. Brown and an American naval officer from the Eastern Mediterranean fleet; I think his name was Mr. Peterson, Mr. Pete Peterson, as I could hear it. Four of us asked to stay here and seven wanted to go back aboard and go to Larnaca on the barge. As I left, I saw Colin Newell coming into the warehouse too, with the British ambassador or counsel. I had told the American counsel that there were some Brits and Canadians, a Spaniard and many Maldive Islanders, etc. on board, and they were able to get all of them help as a result. (My one act which could help others get off that boat would be my one consolation that night.) I was so concerned that there was no one to help all those young students from the Maldive Islands who were on the S.S. Edy. I wanted to help them get home, once they got to Larnaca. The

American Counsel assured me he would get the twenty-seven kids from the Madives some help. They were so dear; I didnn't realize that I was so obsessed with their situation in that warehouse though.

When it was time to leave the port of Haifa, after the negotiations for our release were done and we were searched for the final time, the American Counsel called for a taxi to take us to Tel Aviv where his office was located. When the taxi arrived, I was quite shocked when Mr. Brown asked us each for ten dollars in order to pay for our taxi ride to get to Tel Aviv. One of the students Karen Hajj did not have any money. But I had a twenty-dollar bill so gave it to the counsel so both of us could be taken in the taxi with the counsel to Tel Aviv. I was brought to the consulate in Tel Aviv, nearly fifty miles south of Haifa and helped to make a collect call to home and to my parents' home. No one was home to answer the phone at either place, so I left a message at my sister Patty's to try to contact my family tonight to say where I was and that I was alive and o.k. I can't wait two more hours to try to call them when they return from wherever they are.

I am now in a dive of a hotel (found for me by the consulate, but at my own expense, as with all else). This place was chosen for me because it is the cheapest place and the American consulate did not know if I had any money. I am going to shower and then sleep until nine in the morning. I am still very scared, even here, I want to go home and they will try to get me a direct flight on Tuesday morning, they said. I am so sorry you were not home when I called. I tried on the way to Tel Aviv, just to think of you. It was difficult.

9:20 a.m.

I have slept for six hours and feel better. Now I will get dressed and get a little breakfast. There is a little meal that comes with the room.

The two men who met us when we got off the boat in Haifa were a Mr. Pete Peterson and a Mr. James Hughes, III. The first one is the naval attaché and the other one must be the American Consul. Jim did all the work of getting us off the barge and welcoming us. Both of their wives were also there, but we did not meet them. He said it had been a long day. He had had a long day because the State Department in Washington, D.C. blew up when our ship was captured by the Israelis and they found out that there were captured Americans. He had had quite a long and tough day with the negotiators, he told us. Anyway, four or five Americans who stayed on the ship were going to Jordan and King Hussain was sending a jet to get them from Larnaca and take them to Jordan; those Americans did not want to miss the ride for sure.

I have to pay for everything here in Israel. Thank God I still have some money. I thought the American consulate would help us out, but no luck. I'll spend all of my cash (or a good lump of it anyway). I can't decide why the American consulate won't spend a nickel on us to help us; after all, we are refugees of war. I suspect that they don't want to create any paper record that acknowledges that we Americans were captured by Israel and threatened with being killed at this point in time, and so they simply treat us as tourists at the Consulate.

I am suffering from exhaustion now, and I don't want to go back to work for a while. I am so odd inside - I hurt so much from what I had to see and feel. I want it all to go away, and I have to talk it out with someone pretty soon.

9:50 a.m.

I just downed a breakfast buffet of cheese, a hard-cooked egg, some bread, a piece of orange and some tomato. There is instant coffee, but that is o.k. by me at this point. A Miss Susan Jacobs at the Consulate will help us to get airline tickets and I think that I will fly to Paris, then onto to Dulles all in one day, hopefully tomorrow. I will give her my old ticket in case she can exchange it.

The security to get in and out of this country is stupendous. A full search, body search, even a look at papers and a look into the wallets. The exit at the airport will take at least two hours, we have been told.

While waiting for the American consul to investigate our passports and get us off the ship last night, about two and a half hours of waiting passed. I spent much of it with the soldiers, shooting the bull. They were very dear and kind, by and large. One gets out of the navy as a lieutenant after his four years, this Friday, and he can't wait. He wants to come to New York City to visit his relatives and to study. Another one who is wearing a T-shirt, khakis and sandals, gets out in three months, and he too was very dear. He was aware of how the "s... hit the fan" over the detainment of our ship. He knew we would get off the ship too, if we wanted. I teased them both about their weaponry and boots and equipment, since it was my tax dollars that paid for it. They were sheepish and embarrassed because, on the one hand, they were proud of the modern and topnotch things they had, but, on the other, they knew they came from America and that they had used it all to detain us. I enjoyed reminding them all of this, but I was also ashamed to know that they had killed thousands in the past week with this military technology.

As it turns out, the four students that were taken from the S.S. Edy during the night by the Israelis all had some kind of Palestinian background. One was an American medical student who was also our leader and spokesman for the ship. (Dr. Freyha chose him to be our leader so we would have just one spokesman if approached or boarded). Well, he was a bit of a basket case when they returned him; he was intimidated and quite neurotic - afraid that they would kill him. When we disembarked here last night, he was terrorized, and, when they released him, he went right to the airport to await any flight out of Israel. He called his father to wire him a prepaid ticket out. I've never seen true paranoia before. I suspect he and his family are activists of some sort, and it was only his American passport that saved his life.

Besides this medical student and the other student Karen Hajj, the other American was a businessman who was trying to get back to his office in Greece. He went directly to the airport too.

I shed a few tears at breakfast a few minutes ago. I just could not stop them. But I wasn't crying. They just came.

I will try to call home again today. Right now everyone is still asleep. I will awaken them all, however, with the call. But I will wait until I know my flight number and arrival time.

7:55 p.m.

I went to the Consulate at 10:45 a.m. with Karen Hajj, the other American student who stayed here with me, to seek consulate assistance. We were first interviewed by the naval attaché Captain Pete Peterson who wanted to know all the processes by which we left Junieh and our boat trip and encounter with the Israelis. How did they approach the ship? When? How often? What did they do and say? Et cetera. Karen and I talked a lot and the process of recounting the past hours felt very good. We were nervous to talk at first, but, once we started, it was easy.

Then we got some money exchanged, filled out a form (For what? I don't know.), and then we got our plane tickets made. I got a ticket with a layover in New York City for five and a half hours. I'll try to do much better and call you from NYC if I can.

I tried to call home again, but without any success. So we had some lunch with the American Consul Jim and his wife Carol and their son David - all employees of the consulate here. (David is a sophomore at the University of Virginia when he is not here on his summer job with Daddy.) I had a cheeseburger with mayonnaise, fries and a vanilla shake. It was an all-American thrill, I must admit, and I enjoyed it greatly.

Then I called home again at 2:45 p.m. and heard a friendly voice! I lost my control as I tried to speak; I'm sorry that I could not speak at first. Now I'll be able to see them later tomorrow tonight face-to-face. I was glad that they all knew I was o.k., but sorry they did not know where I was. They did not know if I was in friendly or in enemy hands here in Israel. Well, it is fine. Here they are dependent on U.S. support for about all they do here, especially for military assistance. I am treated well here and really needed to stay and unravel a day.

The Consul gave Karen and me each two of his Jerusalem pottery mugs because he knew these were what we wanted as souvenirs. We wanted to go out shopping, but he felt it was not safe for us, except for a short walk nearby. That was his motivation for the gift - to compensate for the fact we could not go out shopping. But he was kind and I will always remember his wonderful Jewish face, long red beard, and beer-barrel chest.

Karen and I then took our money and went for the short walk about four. We did more than we were supposed to, for about three hours. We found Tel Aviv's shopping district a good place to shop, with low prices for crafts, leather, hand-made clothes, etc. I bought a small handbag for tomorrow so I could check my luggage. Later I went into a leather shop and found another one I liked even better. So I bought that one too. It was a great deal at $24. I think I could have gotten even a better price if I knew how to negotiate better. Karen bought a beautiful crocheted and cloth dress for $14; I think she would have been willing to pay $100 for it in the U.S. Then we decided to eat in our rooms and bought food, first two sweet peaches (different from the ones in Virginia), four fresh figs, and nearly a kilo of green grapes. Then we went into a grocery store for a long French bread loaf and some grapefruit drink. At the room, I dug out a small packet of peanut butter and a piece of cheese I had been hoarding in my bag. I had a pack of instant coffee to drink. We got some hot water and a knife from the little hotel manager and made a feast in one room. We finally relaxed and felt civil and safe.

We were about a half block from the beach, and we sat there for twenty minutes before supper. I took Karen's picture on the beach and she took mine in front of the hotel entrance. I hope she sends me a copy of them. We laughed for the moment and we relaxed.

It was good to have this day here. I was so terrified yesterday that I still was scared this morning, just afraid of everything. I am so accustomed to not knowing what is going to happen next or who to trust, that I couldn't relax. But I did at suppertime. I am all packed and ready to go tomorrow too. We arranged for a taxi to come at 4:45 a.m. There is the two-hour search at the airport so we have to be very early in order to get on the flight.

I don't ever want to experience anything in my life like these past eleven days. I shall be frightened for the rest of my life when I remember this. I wonder why I was given the opportunity to have this amazing set of experiences?

Tuesday, June 15, 1982

4:25 a.m.

I got up at four to shower before catching the 4:45 taxi, but I am too tired today. So I have to be seen this way today. I am all packed and eager. I checked on the taxi and got a cup of instant coffee in the lobby.

I really want to see everybody badly, the family and all the friends because I have felt so all alone. I need to share so much with you all. Also at the same time, I am afraid to see you and to return there because I'll have to talk about it all, and I don't want to talk about everything yet. I'm not ready for work yet either.

5:55 a.m.

We got to the airport easily to make our flight and we were not searched or given the normal treatment. Our tickets were stamped: "Involuntarily rerouted due to political situation," and this gave us very good treatment, I think.

I see that we made the Tuesday morning *Jerusalem Post* (Vol. L, #1554) with a small article on page two which read as follows: *Navy Diverts Lebanese Passenger Ship to Haifa: Tel Aviv*

The Israeli navy intercepted a Lebanese passenger ship as it left Beirut on Sunday and forced it to dock in Haifa, the Army spokesman has announced.

No further details were given, but Israel television said nationals friendly to Israel among the 150 passengers were freed to come ashore or leave Israel for their final destinations.

Their embassies have been informed, it said.

T.V. did not say why the ship was seized and did not identify it.

Note: It's not correct on date and place, but correct choice of the word "seized."

9:20 a.m., in flight

We just had the hugest meal I have ever had on a plane. Even I could not eat it all, and I am hungry. There was a little Jewish lady beside me who kept shoving her things from her food tray onto mine too: "Men can eat more than women; take this," she said. I said, "No, thanks," and put it back on her tray. But she put it back on mine. She is dear, of Czechoslovakian descent, survived the Holocaust and came to Israel in 1947. She is on her way to see her son in San Mateo, California.

Here is what the breakfast was: sliced grapefruit and orange, strawberry yogurt cup, roll and butter, cheese, orange juice, omelet, sliced beef, potato buds, and coffee. Is that not a huge meal for a breakfast!? It was good except for the eggs which were white and hard and dry.

Thoughts of Israel: People don't smile; soldiers all over; very clean, wide, flat and fertile coastal plain; totally Jewish; modern and a nice place to visit but I would not want to live there.

10:55 a.m.

Can you believe I have not run in three days and I'll not for at least another! My taxes are also due today. Also, I have in my suitcase some tax returns from people in Lebanon that are due today. They asked me to bring them to the states and mail them. I will try and get them out of my bag in NYC, and mail them so they'll be postmarked on time.

We are due in Paris at noon with a one and a quarter hour layover. I will try to get a good connection, and call home if I have time.

1:05 p.m.

We arrived in Paris at noon, as scheduled, and are now on board a 747 for New York. I have discovered a flight to D.C. that is nearly four hours earlier than the one on which I am booked.

Later ...

I just rented head phones and guess I will watch the movie *Taps* in order to kill some time. ("Kill some time." That is an odd thing to write.) The flight is seven hours long with a meal and a snack so I'll need something to do besides eat and rest and write in this diary. I'm so excited!

I spent my entire time in the terminal helping the frightened little Jewish lady who was trying to feed me before. She was afraid of the electronic moving walk, the escalators, and much else. So I helped her get in and out of line, and to experience the terror of a moving sidewalk. She was so frightened - only ever flew once before, I think, to see her son's marriage in the United States four years ago.

I hope I'll be able to get an earlier flight in New York. I can't wait an extra minute now!

3:20 p.m.

Maybe my harrowing experience during this past time was meant to provide me and my friends with some important experiences for personal and spiritual growth. I have changed so much, once again, but maybe they will have too. I am scared they will be so angry at me for how much I have hurt them because of all the trauma they experienced back home. It is hard to remember about loving and being loved just now. I know it is alright for people to feel hate or anger toward me sometimes, but just now I dread that possibility.

I've been thinking about reunion with my family for days, ever since Sunday night when I could finally think about the future and have some faith that it would occur. I always become fixated on the thoughts of my reunion, after I have been gone for a time. In my travel diaries from the past three trips, I write about it, about this same point in time too. It will be another twelve and a half hours if I don't find an earlier flight. I expect it will be very emotional and I look forward to it being so. I've got so much inside of me that I need to let it out, but not alone, and not quite yet.

I am not afraid of anything today. I am not expecting anyone to torment me or hurt me. I feel in control of myself and my life.

I saw in a newspaper that early estimates of Lebanese casualties in the past eleven days were estimated as near 10,000 dead and 17,000 casualties. The estimates are expected to soar too. It started me to cry, but I stopped it as I had to. I got a copy of this morning's *Jerusalem Post* for all to see back home, though. I will always want to keep it.

I wonder if the incident made the news in the United States. We don't think so since it was not the only such incident, we've learned. And Mr. Brown, the Consul, told us it would never be reported officially in the United States (although we were free to talk about it). In Tel Aviv, Karen and I were wishing that it was in the news in America. (Maybe I'll be interviewed for the Herald Progress at home, or even a Richmond newspaper!)

12:35 p.m. New York time, but 6:35 a.m. in both Beirut and Paris, I think.

I was thinking about how I adjusted to the war in Beirut. I would sit out on the patio, even go running, during the massive bombings and killings. I would just complain about the inconveniences of the constant interruptions due to the shrapnel, shells and bullets, and having to get under a protective area all the time. We were terrified by the jets and bombs, anti-aircraft fire, and sonic booms, but quickly we located all of the safest places with good views of the skies to watch the air fights and aerial bombings. How strange that we acted that way!

However, it did keep me from being able to sleep. I awoke between four and five every morning of the war, and I couldn't rest for the war tension.

Think of all the people still there in all of that war and terrorism. I don't know how they can cope with it all, except as I and others did - by numbing oneself to it, by refusing to accept its reality when it was bad. I think it is the street gunmen on the loose, and the looters that I was most afraid of. As often as I saw them - people, usually kids or teenagers with old machine guns in the streets - I did not show any fear of them. In fact, I walked right past them because they were not real, not for me anyway. Now there are many roaming the streets and looting, etc., I am sure. It was only that moment, when two of them dragged me out of the car when I was trying to escape Beirut, that I was truly afraid. Especially when we were up against the wall.

I was so angry and frightened then. I worked so hard to get out of there. I put in my time, I waited, and was disappointed for three days. And I stood in line with the cavalcade all morning, and just as I got out of the gate they stopped me. How could they do that to me? They were judging me and condemning me to be terrorized, possibly held as a hostage or worse. There are kids like them who are actually killing people, or helping others to kill. I know that, but I cannot internalize it, even though they almost did it to me. And why? I am so angry about that.

I am disappointed in people. How can people be like that? What about love? What happened to them in their lives? Am I just a naive fool creating my cocoon of love among friends so as not to know what the rest of the world feels?

I don't know about all of this, but I need to rethink all I have learned and unlearned since my April retreat, in light of what I've seen and felt these recent weeks. I will come out of this knowing that love is the answer, the only answer, I am sure. But how do I fit the people who hate so badly into my perception of a God who is love? I don't know yet.

Will I be numb when I get home? That is how Karen Hajj is now, totally numb and blasé about all she has seen and all that has happened to her. I worry about her. Yet she is amazed by her own inability to feel anything. She admitted that. I hope she gets it out when she gets home to

Pennsylvania, and is with her parents.

I wish I had listened to my intuition and inner feeling and had not come to Beirut this time. I should have known that it would be a bad trip for me.

2:10 p.m., in NYC

We will land in about an hour. Then I will go through customs and go looking for a flight home. I hope I remember, and have time to dump all my mail from Beirut into a mail box. Some are tax returns which have to be postmarked by today.

We just had a nice snack of bread with slices of chicken and cheese. There was also a rather stale roll, not at all an appetizing snack. No matter. I will eat at home tonight.

I just got Karen's address so I can send her a followup letter, along with the others whose addresses I have. How can I ever forget her! We've been compatriots since Sunday night; she is nice and very mature, considering some of the others I have met on the boat.

I wonder where the boat is, and what all the others are doing on it? I wonder about the three students we left behind in Junieh because they were not allowed to get on the boat. I am worried about the American teachers at AUB too; they are brave and they have to be. Did I write that on the day I left AUB, Dean Haroutune Armenian's apartment on campus had a bullet come through his children's bedroom window about seven a.m. while they were awake and playing inside? How can they cope with that, except there is no choice right now?

I got through customs quickly and bought a ticket and got on, mostly by telling people I was coming from the war zone and could not afford to miss the flight. So here I go and hope my luggage is with me too. I'll call from D.C and try to get a limo or something home. Home, home, here I come.

4:42 p.m.

What a fluke that was in NYC! I arrived and went through customs quickly by telling my story. I rechecked luggage, ran and got a ticket, and ran to the plane. It had just closed, but they let me get on, again, my dear story. So here I come to D.C. I know there are limos to Fredericksburg and Richmond and I will see you all in three or four hours. I feel a bit numb, not even emotional or excited now, just glad it is nearly over.

I never got to say good-by to Karen. I was so rushed to try to get an earlier flight. She'll be fine, I am sure.

I wonder if I'll ever hear from the State Department again. I would think they would follow up on us. Maybe I ought to let them know I made it home and am well too. Mr. Hughes asked us to do that, as I recall.

Maybe I can rent a car at the airport and come home. I wonder if I am fit to drive. I would have to fight the evening traffic around D.C, but I could do that. I'll see when I get there. It would be easier on the family if I rented a car, but a lot harder on me. Well, I guess I will take the limo.

When I get home, I want to start to restudy myself, my spirituality, and renew the positive attitude that I had going when I was in the States in April and May. I also want to schedule a personal retreat for reflection, sing again at church, get a good book to read, relax and think.

I am sorry that I missed the Curcillo retreat this past weekend. It was a real dream for me, a motivator that I thought about in Beirut. Darn! I guess there will be others. But the thoughts of that weekend sustained me, gave me something to look forward to, something to associate with in the United States with my friends.

We are almost in D.C. already; it is a short flight.

6:20 p.m., in D.C.

I arrived here at the airport at 5:15 and ran to get the Groome Limo at 5:30, but I couldn't take it as my bags did not make my flight. So I called home but the line was busy. Now I'll wait for my bags on the next flight at 7:10. I think my family will be here by eight. I hope so.

What the hell! Why be impatient now? I've not been aware of time having meaning for so long that I might as well be unaware of time altogether. I will wait as long as I have to. I want to have a cheeseburger. That's it. I will look around, put in time, and have a very American cheeseburger. After all, this is America!

Later ...

I finally got through on the phone, and told you where I am and of my plans. How silly it was to tell you to bring me some Diet Coke! I don't know what made me think of that, but it is what I was thinking of. You can't get it in Beirut, and I want something that does not exist there, I guess.

Wednesday, June 16, 1982

7:19 a.m.

I'm unpacking, still a bit tense and could only sleep five hours. I am so happy to be home. It feels so good to be loved again. I am so happy.

ORIGINAL EPILOGUE

So much happened to me as a result of my experience in Beirut that I want to give some idea of the extent to which it impacted my life immediately and thereafter. That it totally changed my life must be apparent. That it continued to change my life may not be quite so obvious, but it did. This epilogue is written more for me as a catharsis than for anyone else to read. However, it is hoped that the readers (if there are any) will find it worthwhile, if not as interesting and exciting as the diary itself.

My Arrival at the Airport in D.C.

When I arrived at Washington National Airport on June 16 to await my family, I was numb, somewhere way beyond feeling. Once one gets beyond the level of emotionality where there are tears or laughter or other outbursts, there is a whole range of emotions and feelings that defy description of phenomenal expression. I was somewhere out there.

It was one of those times when I knew my luggage had not made my flight change in New York and, of course, I was right. Waiting the extra couple of hours for my luggage was frustrating, but I was resigned to it and, by then, quite accustomed to waiting. After several hours I had my luggage and, at the other end of the airport room, I saw my friend Paul coming in. I noticed him immediately and caught his attention. He came over and hugged me and took my luggage. We walked out into the parking lot. Coming across the parking lot was his wife walking with mine. I was beyond feeling. I went to my wife who took me and led me to a car to go home. The anticipated emotional outpouring did not (no, could not) occur. An act of love, sent by my friends, a cooler of Diet Coke, was in the back of the car. It is a great addiction of mine.

About midnight we pulled into my driveway after two hours of nondescript small talk. Tied around the large maple tree in the front yard was an enormous yellow ribbon, reminiscent of those displayed during the days of the Iranian crisis in 1980. A huge spotlight shown on it and under the tree were more nested bottles of Diet Coke. I learned that the tree, the spotlight and cola were all arranged as gifts from my friends to welcome me home.

The kids were sleeping when I went in the house, so I did not see them. But I had some phone calls to make. First, I called my mother and told her that I was home; she very coolly and calmly said she was glad and would talk to me after I had relaxed. The one-minute call ended. Then I called my dear friend and singing buddy Hayes, the knowledge of whose friendship sustained me. The phone only rang once when he answered it. I was ecstatic; I was alive and he was happy and we would go on as friends and singers. And then I called Sister Elizabeth Durney, another dear friend who was a counselor and supporter for my family while I was gone. Again the phone rang only once and she knew I was home and all was well.

I went to bed and slept quickly and soundly and was up by seven. It was before nine a.m. when the phone rang. The Richmond newspaper knew I was home and wanted to talk to me. (In the next two weeks I did one newspaper interview and two television interviews, the second of which was a two-part and two-night feature on the news. The experience with the Richmond newspaper was most grueling and I was deeply sorry I talked with them.)

On the very first day of return home, I did a telephone interview with that newspaper. A young girl all too exuberant did the interview. Shortly thereafter, she called back to say that her editor thought I was a hoax, that there were not Americans in Beirut, much less prisoners. Her newspaper was going to send a photographer to the house to take my picture and wanted also to photograph my passport to see my visas of entry to and exit from Israel. I was angry, but I complied. When the photographer arrived, he took a picture of me with my young daughter sitting under the tree with the yellow ribbon, and took the pictures of my passport. I was cold toward him, and he was embarrassed. Several days later when the story finally appeared, it was printed as a human interest story. No mention was made of my captors nor of our treatment in Beirut, at sea or in Israel. The captors were reported as Palestinians. (See pages158-161.)

If there were any benefits in my doing the little bit of public media coverage, it was that it was picked up by Associated Press and given wide coverage. I received a phone call from NBC in New York asking for information as well, but I did not respond. My only interest in doing the two articles (the television and newspaper) was a reason which I made clear to both of the media when they requested it. I wanted to be able to tell my whole story and I wanted them to listen to it, because I was surprised that the newspaper coverage in the United States did not contain much of the reality that was happening in Lebanon.

My First Couple of Weeks at Home

I could not go to work and I could not relax for a couple of weeks. Every plane that went over frightened me, and every loud noise made me jump. Although I was glad to be home, I was scared. I felt guilty that I got out when so many others did not. I was nervous and could not live with myself at times. I was sustained by a flood of love and support from a large community of friends, some of whom I hardly knew before. The notes that were passed to me at home, in church, and by people who met me gave me a sense of love, of acceptance and of support. Numerous phone calls, informal visits and indescribable acts of love seemed to happen daily. I felt loved. I used the expression "Love empowers." to describe my reaction.

I talked a good bit about my diary during these weeks and

how important it was to be writing out my feelings all that time. But I could not bear to read it, although my family was reading it. Everyone said that I should publish it and share my story with others. But I couldn't, because I could not think about it, because I couldn't prepare it. But I knew I had to try someday, but not then.

When the newspaper article was picked up by Associated Press and circulated about the mid-Atlantic states, the phone calls started. They seemed to be constant and, in several days, they were followed by letters. A typical phone call would go like this: "Hello, Dr. Breindel, I heard you just got back from Beirut. My daughter is there, and I've not heard anything from her since the war started. Did you happen to see her? Do you know her? Did you see the house where she lived? Was that house hit?" and so on. I tried to be nice to the callers. I tried to tell them I had only been in Beirut a few weeks, that I didn't know their relatives, and that I was not able to get out and look around the city when the war began and I could not help them. I was always a bit frustrated. They were so disappointed but they were always kind to me too. After a week or two I could not take any more of these calls and so I didn't. Over three months after my return I was still receiving phone calls.

Finally, people started to nag and harangue me about talking to the State Department or my congressman or somebody so that they should know of the experiences of my interactions with the consulates in Beirut and Tel Aviv, and of what some people considered injustices. But I never did contact anyone. It did not seem to be of any value or purpose that I should talk to people. And besides, I could not bear to think about all the details, to deal with the specifics. I wanted to forget it all, and I did not want to remember any more. My over-whelming feeling during these first weeks home was that I wanted it all to go away. Every day I prayed that God would let me go back in time to May and give me another chance to decide whether to go on the trip, and that I would not choose to go. I just wanted it to have not happened to me or anyone else.

Flashbacks

One Saturday afternoon about three weeks after I was back home, I was sitting with a group of people at a party. I had my first "flashback." (It has been recounted earlier in the book, in the original preface.

Two days later I called my friend Sister Elizabeth and asked her to advise me on what had happened to me and where to get help with it. She described the flashback phenomenon to me. She compared it to the experiences that some family members feel at a death, but suppress until later on in the bereavement process when they finally let their feelings come out. It is a sort of delaying process that the brain does when a particular feeling cannot be expressed or felt at the time it occurs. She said I would probably have other flashbacks and that I ought to get used to them, and accept them as a positive way of expending stored-up emotions. If I could keep from being embarrassed at the time, it was a very wholesome process. (I told at the beginning of this book a similar one when I attended a dress rehearsal of the Ice Follies the following week.) These strange re-livings of emotions that I had suppressed in Beirut occurred for about six weeks after I was home. I am now glad they happened, but it was a difficult process in my early time back home.

There was a particularly difficult flashback. The first plane trip I took after coming back from Beirut was in mid-July, about a month later. I was flying to Philadelphia for the day. I was excited to be going to Philadelphia because Karen Hajj, the other American with me in Tel Aviv, lived near where I was going. I was eager to call on her and see if she was doing any better than I was. Well, it must have been thinking of her that did it. After I had been in the plane for a while, I suddenly reverted to being on the plane coming out of Tel Aviv. Although I was flying from Richmond to Philadelphia in reality, in my mind I was flying out of Tel Aviv and I started to feel the release of tension, the joy, the anger, the guilt and all the other strange mixed-up emotions I had on that morning plane to Paris. I cried and cried. Even upon landing and taking the limo to my hotel, I could not seem to get back to reality. Once alone in the hotel room, I lay down on the bed and relived one of my final nights in Beirut (lying on my back in Marquand House and waiting for the early morning air raids to begin). It seemed hours that I lived this Beirut experience. Somehow I finally fell asleep and awoke early the next morning with only a few hours of sleep, back to reality, but frightened by the experience. I made a point after that of never letting myself be alone if I felt a flashback coming on.

The flashbacks finally ended later in 1982. Although the flashbacks were over, periodic feelings caused tears when discussing Beirut for nearly one year.

(Note: The last paragraph was written early in 1983. There were at least two more significant flashbacks, one five years later and another in late 1990. It is now fifteen years since one has occurred.)

Speaking Engagements

Once the school year began in September I was back into my teaching and research and writing. I was not having much luck at any of them. The students asked me to spend my first lecture of the fall semester telling them of my experiences because they had all heard about them informally and they wanted to hear about them from me personally. So I talked to them for an hour and it was a good release for me. It was during the early fall that I started to receive requests, first from the Baptist Men's Breakfast Club and my daughter's junior high school social studies class. Then a private school in Richmond called, and then others, all wanting me to speak about the Middle East, the Israeli invasion of Lebanon, and about my personal experiences in Lebanon the past two years. I accepted some of these invitations and agreed to present a non-political lecture, with discussion of the Middle East and my experiences as I could interpret them. During all of my speaking engagements around Virginia, there were many questions which surprised me, and made me aware of the general naivete of most people about the countries, peoples, and politics of the Middle East. Although I had not become an expert on the region, I had been studying the situation for several years, and now was doing so with gusto and vigor. I had an understanding of the many actors and a sense of the history of the region. It was a gratifying time for me to be able to share with others the basic knowledge of what I thought would become a most important part of the world in my lifetime and theirs. Of course, throughout it all came the regular requests to publish my diary, or some part of my story for others to read. I still could not do that, however.

Reading the Diary

It was about Thanksgiving 1982 that I made up my mind to read my Beirut diary. The occasion of my reading was a commitment I had made to dictate the diary in a slightly edited format so that it could be typed into a readable manuscript. I did it quickly in a couple of days and, throughout the entire process, I was overwhelmed by the emotionality in my diary, by the detail of my personal experiencing of the events of those days, and by the vividness with which I relived each day and activity that I read. I was also quite surprised by the many things that I did not write down, things that did not seem to mean much to me at the moment, but which by then were now very vivid and important to me. Reading the diary aloud was another catharsis for me, a rather deep and thorough one at that. Thereafter, much of the anger and most of the other feelings were gone, or at least minimal. After six months, my constant living in the shadow of Beirut and the war seemed to dissipate and I could move on.

It was shortly after Christmas that I decided to read a part of it again, this time to my dear friend Richie with whom I wanted to share the latter part of the diary. We sat down together in the living room one evening and I began reading to him the story of June 4, the one I wrote on June 5 as a reflection on that first day of war sights and sounds. I was surprised by my tears and my fears as I read it. But I was able to read it and I was able to share it. And I could share it with him because he cared about me, understood me, and was happy for my successful return. After that time, I knew I could share it with anyone because I was not an expendable commodity, because the people around me proved I wasn't and am not.

In time I will be able to put Beirut in a reasonable perspective and appreciate the full consequences of those experiences in God's plan for me. The whole experience taught me how much I wanted to live, how prepared I was to die, and how human I was. The experience of coming home to a community of love and acceptance was something I had never experienced before and which few do. Knowing that the community of support exists, and will always exist, has made the whole experience a positive one in retrospect. I am only sorry that tens of thousands of people had to die as I grew in spirit and understanding. I cannot help but wonder if I am the only one who figured out that there is no such thing as a human life which is an expendable commodity, not mine, nor that of any Lebanese, Syrian, Palestinian or Israeli.

[End of the Original Diary, with its Epilogue]

EPILOGUE

With the passing of time, the events of May and June 1982 in Beirut are now in a better perspective. It is no longer a mystery to me why I lived through those harrowing days in Beirut, nor why I reacted so intensely to them. My own spiritual journey since that summer is easy to track now.

I came back home in a heightened state of being saved from death by a loving God. In my amazement and gratitude, I interpreted that morning's foreboding on June 3 on the green field as a message from God, a God who wanted me to know that he was taking care of me. This wonderful God gave me this saving insight that morning as a way of telling me that he would be taking care of me in the coming days of difficulty, that I need not be afraid because I was being cared for. Although I came to this understanding early after my return from Beirut, I still had the question of why this loving God took care of me when he did not seem to take care of so many others. And even more lingering was the question of what he had saved me for. For what role was he caring for me? What did he want me to be doing with my life, that I was spared from a death in Sidon that afternoon? I wanted to know, and I began to search for an answer. It took a long time to find the answer.

The decade of the eighties brought me into single parent-hood, significant illness, and hard times. The difficulties only affirmed for me, however, that God was taking care of me, and I never lost heart or faith. Just as I needed to experience Beirut and war, I must need to experience these hardships too, I reasoned. Somehow, I told myself that God was shaping me, molding me, and giving me this life, so that I could be prepared for some particular purpose somewhere down the road of life. I never suspected what it would be for a very long time. And when it became clear to me that I was to use the life experiences I had been given as a minister of the Gospel of Jesus, I was thunderstruck. I did not believe it! I would not believe that all those years, all those pains, all those people with so many difficulties, were preparing me to serve the people of God as an ordained Catholic priest.

The acceptance came slow at first. I did not want to be a priest, and I certainly did not want to give up all that I had accumulated in the late eighties and nineties - great job, world traveling, status, family, material success, and more. I did not want to give any of it up. That is, I did not want to give it up until the same voice which spoke to me on the green field on June 3, 1982 told me to change. "Follow me." (Luke 5:27)

Once I recognized the voice, I recognized the messenger. And I changed and happily so. After all that was the lesson I learned in Beirut. Once you know what God wants, once you feel God's presence in your life, what else can you do but follow and obey, with the sure knowledge of his loving care?

If God took care of me in Beirut, he would take care of me as a priest no matter where I was.

The Last of the Flashbacks

The flashbacks which occurred during the early days back from Beirut left me after the first few months. But there were two hidden deep inside me somewhere. It had been over five years since I came back from Beirut, and I was catching a plane in Washington National Airport (now, Reagan International Airport) in 1988. I had not been in that airport terminal since the day I arrived back from Beirut. But, until it occurred, I did not recall this. Not until the flashback came. There I was at the airport, rushing down a corridor to my gate when I began to sob uncontrollably. It was six years since I ran down those look-alike corridors, yet there I was, in my mind, arriving home from Beirut, after those weeks of thinking I would never be home again. I was on American soil, and I was so very grateful in my disbelief. I was coming home. I was safe. I made it back when so many did not. I could not stop crying. Maybe the calendar read 1988, but it was June 1982 for me. And I made it out! How I wept! I had never felt such joy in my whole life.

I don't know why I could not feel this joy when I came down that corridor in 1982. I am so very grateful I could finally feel it though.

At the onset of the gulf war in Kuwait in 1990, I went after work to the blood donor center to give blood. As I lay in the donor chair, the first scenes in black-and-white from the bombing of Baghdad were being shown on the television screens in front of us donors. I watched in horror the scenes of the night skies with the silhouetted minarets and mosques, the flashes of anti-aircraft guns and the gray clouds of bursting bombs. I wept quietly. I did not know why at first. I did not know anyone in Baghdad; I had no loved ones in the fight. Yet I sobbed and whimpered in silence as the blood flowed from me. I was not in Richmond, Virginia, as I wept, I came to realize. Not in my heart and mind. It had been nearly a decade, 8.5 years to be exact. But I was in Beirut, on the terrace of Marquand House, and I was watching the night sky, and anticipating being bombed and killed. I was hearing the sounds of bombs and guns and killing and death in Beirut.

The staff of the blood center came to me, gave me tissues, said nothing to me, but muttered to each other something about my relatives who must be in Baghdad. When I got up from the donor chair, I got in my car and drove quickly to a friend's home nearby. I pounded on the door and, when she opened it, I pushed past her and ran to the doorway to the basement. I stood in the safety of this inner door until I could stop crying. I was amazed at myself - I knew to find an inner doorway for safety, and to stay there during a bombing raid!

The bombing ceased in my heart and mind, but not in Baghdad, that afternoon. That was the last flashback. But there was one more very difficult emotion to expend. It came the next year.

It was hard to feel happy about having gotten home safely from Beirut. I could not understand that feeling of sadness when I recalled my coming home from Beirut. I should have been happy, even excited, but I never was (at least not after the first initial period). Thereafter, I could not stand to listen to the news of Lebanon, to hear of the real hostage-taking and to read the papers or listen to the news. In the mid-1980s I stopped watching television altogether and I canceled my daily newspaper. I refused to know the news. I did not want to think of Beirut, the Middle East, and all the media coverage being given to hostage-takers and warmongers. But I did not know why I felt this way. Not until the first week of December 1991.

On Monday, December 2, 1991 American hostage Joseph Cicippio was released in Lebanon. On Tuesday, December 3, 1991 American hostage Alan Steen was released. (And on Wednesday, December 4, 1991, the longest held and the last hostage Briton Terry Waite was released.) I heard on the early morning news as I dressed for work that Tuesday morning that Alan would be released. I was happy for him and his family, I recalled thinking. I got ready and drove to the University where I was to teach a graduate class in health services management. I was not conscious of my thinking of Alan Steen. Only a few minutes into my lecture, I put down my notes, and I told the students about Mr. Steen, and how there were now no more American hostages in Lebanon. And, just as I did in my flashbacks, I began to weep. But this time the weeping brought tears of joy, intense joy. Not for Alan Steen, but for me. At last, I could be happy. At last I could rejoice in my freedom. I could be happy because I did not have to also feel guilty about getting out of there when so many others did not. For over nine years, I withheld my joy at my freedom, I realized, because I felt so guilty about being free when others were not. But now, on December 3, 1991, nine years, six months, and 18 days later, I too was free, truly free, to forget the past, with its pain, its guilt and its joys. I was now free to begin to move forward to my new life.

Within a month I resolved to follow the call of my God and made plans to begin study for the priesthood. I had only to complete the work of raising my last children. I entered seminary in summer 1996, as planned, shortly after my last daughter and last foster son were graduated from high school. I do not look back any more. I will never look backward again.

Charles and youngest daughter, Tressa, on the morning
of his safe return home.

[Photo by Tommy Price, Richmond NewsLeader, June 21, 1982.]

Correspondence and Other Referenced Materials,
Back at Home in the USA

The Richmond News Leader, Monday, June 21, 1982, p.11

Doctor makes narrow escape from Beirut
By Carol O'Connor Wolf, News Leader Staff Writer

Dr. Charles L. Breindel said that when he was dodging bullets and shrapnel in Lebanon last week, he didn't think he would make it home for Father's Day.

But tonight, Dr. Breindel said, there will be a "most joyous Father's Day celebration" when he, his wife Josie, and their four daughters are together for the first time since he left May 24 to teach a three-week course at the American University of Beirut.

Dr. Breindel, 41, is an Ashland resident and a professor of health sciences at the Medical College of Virginia.

'TO SEE THE SHOW'

He said that when the Israeli invasion began on June 6, a Sunday, most people went outside or looked out of windows "to see the show."

"Once we realized, however, that those Israeli planes were dropping real bombs, the 'show' ceased to be fascinating. I was scared. It was so macabre that I was in danger of being killed by U.S. weapons sold to Israel," he said.

Dr. Breindel said he spent the next nine days making telephone calls, listening to the sounds of bombs dropping, worrying and hoping that "somehow, someway I was going to be able to escape from this madness and get home."

He said officials at the American University "really were concerned and did everything they could to get us out of there safely."

Their efforts and his eventually paid off. Dr. Breindel arrived at Washington National Airport at midnight last Tuesday. He didn't return to Richmond until late Wednesday "because they lost my baggage. At that point, however, it didn't really matter."

"After the American Embassy pulled out on Monday, I and other

Americans were stranded," he said in describing his efforts to escape Lebanon, a country that is smaller than Connecticut. All we could do was sit around and pray we didn't get hit with shrapnel."

Escaping was made more difficult when the Beirut airport, occupied by the Palestinian Liberation Organization, was bombed. "It wasn't like I could just go over and buy a ticket on the next plane home. That was the country's only airport," he said.

That left just two ways to get out of the country. "We knew we either had to go on the overland road to Damascus or we had to get out by sea. Later on Tuesday, we found out that the road to Damascus had been closed. We knew then that we had to get to Port Juniyah," in Lebanon.

The constant bombing was "making us all crazy and by Wednesday I was going wild. That was when I cabled my family and told them that I couldn't get out. That it just wasn't safe."

On Thursday, driven by desperation, Dr. Breindel said he and the other professors and students took two cattle trucks and a couple of cars owned by the university and piled in - their destination was Juniyah.

It was also on Thursday, he said, that the Israelis dropped yellow leaflets in Beirut saying that there were only two or three hours to get out before massive bombing would begin.

FORCED TO RETURN

As the caravan left the city, Dr. Breindel said his vehicle was stopped by Palestinians. Because he was an American, he said, he was forced to return to the university campus. "I was really worried. I thought I was done for, and I remember thinking that I just couldn't let my knees go out from me. Not then."

Finally, "a very brave man named 'Omar' came to the university and got me and two other visiting professors. We headed straight to the port and met up with the others."

By the time they arrived, the Israelis had blockaded Juniyeh, he said. Friday came and went. On Saturday, "we were told a boat had been *negotiated - the S.S. Edy, a 50-year old cargo ship. Our entire group was loaded onto the boat and we set sail at 10-12 knots for Larnaca, Cyprus."*

In the middle of the night, the Edy was approached by a gunboat; Dr Breindel said he still isn't sure of the vessel's nationality.

"The captain (of the Edy) and one of the passengers who has [sic] been designated as a spokesman were ordered to come onto their ship. They spent about ninety minutes before they came back. We didn't know if we would get our captain back," he said.

"They left us alone at that point. Later, though, they came back and wanted all students of Syrian extraction. It was so frightening to have people yanked out of our midst. Young people. It was craziness," he said.

'BEEN GOING IN CIRCLES'

The students were returned the next morning and it was at that time that "we discovered we had been going in circles. We were no closer to Cyprus than we had been when we started."

After relinquishing all photographic equipment and film, the group was allowed to continue to the port of Haifa in Israel where Dr. Breindel and his fellow Americans were greeted by the American consulate.

"I was so thrilled when I learned that the consulate wanted to see our passports on Sunday. I jumped overboard. When I think about this now, I'm surprised that I did something like that."

Breindel's joy and appreciation of being home are tempered by the realization that there are "many, many more Americans still unaccounted for."

"Our neighbors have been wonderful to us and the people at our church, St. Anne's Catholic Church, have been so wonderful and helpful. Without them, my wife and children would have really been going through some terror," he said.

[This article appeared in the Richmond News Leader, the former afternoon paper of Richmond. The Richmond Times-Dispatch now holds the copyright to the News Leader material. The article is used with permission to reprint the story, and any publication fee was waived.]

Note: I was not 41 years old, but 34. I did not say the PLO were at the airport, nor that Palestinians were the ones who took me from the escape car. I also was quite aware that the vessel which stopped the S.S. Edy was an Israeli submarine. I did not jump overboard in Haifa. There were other discrepancies between what I reported and what was written. I was angry about the article and would not consent to any more interviews.

The article was picked up by Associated Press and ran throughout the region on June 22, 1982. I was forwarded copies from The Ledger-Star, Norfolk, Virginia; The Free-Lance Star, Fredericksburg, Virginia; Roanoke Times & World News; Daily News Record, Harrisonburg, Virginia; and Winchester Evening News.

June 18, 1982

Nabil M. Kronfol, M.D.
Chairman, HSA
Faculty of Health Sciences
101 Van Dyke Building
American University of Beirut
Beirut, LEBANON

Dear Nabil,

I hope you've received my cable which I sent to you, Haroutune, and President Dodge to say that I returned safely to the U.S. on Tuesday night, after a long and crazy departure from Lebanon by way of Haifa port and Tel Aviv.

Thank you for your assistance and support of me during my recent stay. I do hope that you are all safe and comfortable; I worry about you so.

I am returning the unused portion of my AUB ticket (both original and hastily prepared one for the Cyprus trip). I did not use it, due to our seizure by the Israel navy and my escape at Haifa port. You will want to get back the cash value of it. At the same time, I am requesting financial assistance from AUB to cover my alternative travel back to the states. Although the U.S. Embassy helped me get off the ship and arranged super-saver tickets, I had to bear the return costs of $735 from the trip as follows:

Airfare Tel Aviv to NYC	$529.00
Airfare NYC to DC	116.00
Taxis in Tel Aviv	32.00
Meals in transit (Thursday to Tuesday) about	35.00
TOTAL	$735.00

Please advise me of your arrangements in this regard. I have enclosed receipts for the airfare for your records.

May you remain in safety and comfort. I look forward to hearing from you soon.

Sincerely,

Chuck (signature)
Charles L. Breindel, Ph.D.
Assistant Professor

Copy: Haroutune Armenian, Dean
      David Dodge, President

American University of Beirut
Beirut, Republic of Lebanon
September 20, 1982

Dear Chuck:

Just a short note to tell you that I have indeed received your
June 18 letter along with the ticket stubs. We are processing
payment through the Business Office. You must realize that
things are not running smoothly over here. We are trying our
best however. Keep well and hope to see you in the future
again over here in this martyred land.

We are all well, thank God. Harout, Eva, Nadim and the
MPH students join me in sending you warm regards.

Nabil M. Kronfol, MD., Dr.PH
Associate Professor and Chairman
Health Services Administration

June 22, 1982

Mr. Colin Newell
25 Cleveland Gardens
London, W2 ENGLAND

Dear Colin,

As I left the port of Haifa by cab, I saw the British consul come to shore with you and the Australian, and I was glad to see you depart the S.S. Edy, I found our American consul very friendly and helpful, but poor; I even had to pay for my own taxi ride to Tel Aviv to the Embassy that night. I spent Monday in Tel Aviv with Karen Hajj, the American AUB student. The other Americans, Tony (went off to his GM office) and Paul (headed directly for the Airport), left the Embassy on their own. I found a flight to the U.S. on Tuesday morning and arrived home by midnight. Now I'm exhausted, and enjoying some slow living for a couple of days.

I've enclosed a copy of the newspaper picture, but it is not very good. Hope it serves its purpose however. Your friends will enjoy it as you tell your story of the great escape.

Thank you so much for your friendship and support, first, during our stay together at Marquand House, and second, while we escaped and endured. I will always remember you fondly and recall our AUB experiences together. I hope you were able to relax for a few days before going back to work.

Please give my warm regards to Marie-Louise. I look forward to hearing from you.

Sincerely,

Chuck (signature)
Charles L. Breindel, Ph.D.
Assistant Professor

25 Cleveland Gdns
London W.2. U.K.
Wednesday 23rd June 1982

Dear Chuck,

Well, I made it back home eventually, probably at about the same time as you. It is really good to be back!

Shortly after you and the other Americans had left the Edy in Haifa, I went to sleep, but I was awakened a short while later to be told that one of the Israeli commanders wanted to see me. He told me he had obtained permission to allow the Britons on the boat to leave in the same way as the Americans. So two of us, me and the Black and Decker salesman from Athens, and his Australian friend, jumped into the same boat that you had left on, and went ashore. The Edy was just being refueled at that time and I have no knowledge of what happened to her subsequently. We were searched and taken to a couple of offices where we filled in the appropriate forms and got our visas. The British Consul and an Air Attache were there. Apparently they had been told about us at about 9 p.m. (It was then about midnight) through a private tip off from the American Consul, I think, and they had driven up to Haifa, not knowing whether there were two or twenty-two of us aboard. The Consul was a tremendous big enebriated (sic) Glaswegian dressed in jeans, sweatshirt and training shoes. The Air Attache was just the opposite, dressed in uniform, formal with a superb upper class military accent. We left Haifa about 45 minutes after leaving the boat and drove to Tel-Aviv where the Consul put us up in his home for the night. It was luxury to have a shower and a bed to sleep in.

The next morning we went to the Consulate, sent off telexes, organised flights, and booked into the Tel-Aviv Sheraton. Later that day, after a sleep we went for a drink or two, then out to an open-air fish restaurant by the shore. My flight to London left Ben Gurion at about 10:30 the next morning, after I had amused the security about my mode of arrival in the country, and I arrived safely at Heathrow to be met by a very relieved and happy Marie-Louise. She seems to have been the centre of a big network of communications sending news about me all over the place.

After a couple of days good sleeping, eating, telling friends about everything, and trying to get back to normal at work and at home, I embarked on another long journey in a boat.   Marie-Louise and I travelled (sic) across to the Netherlands on Thursday night, taking the night boat from Dover, which only takes 5 hours so it is not worth (or possible) to get a berth. So I've had enough nights on boats in the last week or two to satisfy me for a long time. We had a fine weekend there, meeting some of her 8 brothers and sisters, their spouses, and some of their 23 children, and, of course, her parents who turned out to be rather formidable, more aloof and silent and formal, than aggressive and forward.

Now, having been back at work for a couple of days, I am just really beginning to get back to normal, to feel as if London is real, and to begin to think of my experiences of the last week or two in some kind of perspective.

Anyway, how did you get on after you left us? I am going to write to Prakash now and see how he got on on his way to Cyprus and home.

I look forward to hearing now you made your way home,

Regards,

Colin

June 22, 1982

Robert Norton, Ph.D.
Department of Education
Yarmouk University
Irbed, JORDAN

Dear Bob,

I was delighted to disembark from the S.S. Edy that night in Haifa and, after a day of interviews and rest in Tel Aviv, to return home to the states late Tuesday night. I am amazed by the extent of my physical and nervous exhaustion now. It was a strange and unbelievable experience and I have not internalized it yet, but I'm doing okay.

I do hope that you are well and have also returned safely and comfortably to your family. I will always recall you fondly as my co-American who was removed from the Junieh caravan, and a thoughtful and kind friend to me and the students during our several days of existence in the port and on the S.S. Edy.

May God reward your kindness with kindness. I have enclosed a copy of the newspaper picture. Although it is not good, I hope it enlivens your tales of our departure - or attempted departure - from AUB on Thursday June 10.

Give my warm regards to your wife and son. I look forward to hearing from you as you can write.

Sincerely,
Chuck (signature)
Charles L. Breindel, Ph.D.
Assistant Professor

June 22, 1982

Mr. Omar M. Faour
c/o Ms. Mary Bajada
P.O. Box 2987 - AUB
AUB Office

Dear Mr. Faour,

Thank you for your wonderful assistance on Thursday June 10, 1982 when you drove us to the Museum in order to help us leave AUB for Junieh and the departure ship to Larnaca, Cyprus. I shall always remember you for your important role in my return.

May you be blessed for your kindnesses. I am enclosing my half of the 300 Lebanese pounds which you loaned us. You'll receive the other half from Dr. Norton soon if you have not already.

I hope that you and your family are safe.

Sincerely,

Chuck (signature)
Charles L. Breindel, Ph.D.
Assistant Professor

June 22, 1982

Pakash C. Gupta
Dental Research Section
Tala Institute of Fundamental Research
Homi Bhabha Road
Bombay 400005
INDIA

Dear Prakash,

By now you are back safely at home with your family. I hope that you are well and happy, despite our unusual experiences and frightening departure from Lebanon. I arrived home at midnight Thursday, June 15. It was so nice to see my family, but I was very tired - both physically and psychologically.

I have photocopied the pictures from the newspaper which I got in Junieh. It is not good, but I think it will be okay for enlivening your story of our escape.

I enjoyed our time together, despite the circumstances. I appreciate your friendship and kindness to me too; you will always remain special in my memories. My daughter thanks you for the Indian coins too.

Please keep in touch from time to time.

Sincerely,

Chuck (signature)
Charles L. Breindel, Ph.D.
Assistant Professor

Letters from Prakash Gupta

Letter #1, with two newspaper enclosures, arrived shortly after he arrives back in Bombay

Dr. P.C. Gupta
T.I.R.F.
Dental Section
Bombay 400005

Dear Chuck,

It was a pleasure to receive your letter and xerographic copy of the newspaper photograph. I arrived in Bombay on Thursday, 17th June morning, safe and well but as you mentioned yourself, extremely tired emotionally as well as physically.

We started from Haifa after midnight and as you might be knowing, along with Americans, all the Britishers including Colin also got down at Haifa. The journey to Larnaca took about 24 hours. The next day was slightly rougher as many persons on the freighter got sick. It was a joy to touch the solid earth after a long, long way the next morning. Getting used to waiting helped at every stage and I was in a hotel in Larnaca by the evening with a confirmed reservation to Bombay for the next day. As a grand finale to the adventurous trip, in Bombay I found that the airline had lost my suitcase but fortunately it was recovered within a week.

I am enclosing a newspaper account which is slightly dramatic, of my interview, and an original cutting from the daily Cyprus Mail. I think you might be interested in having this picture but please do send me a copy as on our xerox machine the copy is not good.

Looking back it is clear that all of us did pass through difficult times. In making many of those moments lighter and even to some extent enjoyable, your contribution was quite significant, for me as well as I think, for many others.

With warm regards and best wishes,

Yours sincerely,

Prakash (signature)
Prakash C. Gupta
Dental Research Section

Enclosure#1

The Daily, Monday, June 21, 1982
Indian's Nightmare in Lebanon
'Sorry, we can't help you!'

Bombay, June 20 (PTI)

SOLDIERS, barricades and the continuous crump of artillery shells, in short are the ingredients that make up a nation at war. This was how Dr. P.C. Gupta, a scientist at the TIFR here described the eight weeks he spent in turbulent Lebanon.

Dr. Gupta told PTI that he had gone to the American University of Beirut in Lebanon to give courses in epidemiology and also for some "collaborative research work." Never did he believe that he would be caught in the crossfire of a nation facing aggression and torn apart by civil war.

On June 6, all examinations at the University were canceled - Israelis had invaded Lebanon in massive force and there was a danger to life on the campus.

On Thursday, June 10, a group of four visiting professors, including Dr. Gupta and 150 students, embarked on trucks and cars with a military escort to the Port of Jouniyah, in the Christian half of Beirut. However, their intention to proceed by ship to Larnaca in Cyprus was prevented by the Israelis who blocked the waterways.

However, intervention by the American University authorities and the US Embassy in Israel, finally persuaded the Israelis to grant permission for the SS Eddy to leave Jouniyah, with its complement of academics.

But barely half-an-hour later, an Israeli patrol boat intercepted the vessel, and ordered it to Haifa Harbour. The ship tacked, passing devastated Sidon and Tyre - their skies aglow with the fury of conflict.

At Haifa, after a perfunctory (sic) interrogation - they asked a few simple questions - the Americans and Britons were released on the intervention of their embassies. Dr. Gupta was not so fortunate.

"India has no diplomatic ties with Israel - sorry we can't help you." After a thorough search of the vessel, the ship departed for Larnaca, reaching at 6 that evening. So ended Dr. Gupta's adventure.

Glad to be back home, Dr. Gupta said that he was still troubled by recurrent dreams of artillery and aircraft fire. "When an aircraft passes, I instinctively tense for the sound of anti-aircraft fire."

Enclosure #2

Cyprus Mail, Vol.124, No. 12, 412
Wednesday, June 16, 1982

600 evacuees arrive in Cyprus

Another 600 evacuees from Lebanon arrived at Larnaca yesterday, most of them foreign nationals, and many of them have already left to their home countries.

They were transported in two vessels, the Italian naval vessel "Nave Carole" which landed 457 persons of whom 100 were Italians and the others were Americans, British, Swedes, Swiss, W. Germans, Lebanese, and four Cypriots, and the Lebanese craft

"Eddy" with 147 people, mostly Lebanese and foreign students.

The arrival of the Italian vessel had been announced before and the Italian Ambassador Mr. Toscano and Italy's Hon. Consul in Cyprus Mr. Tony Mantovani were at Larnaca harbour when it landed its passengers.

A detachment of commandos presented arms as the Ambassador went on board together with the Hon. Consul.

Representatives of the Red Cross were also at the port to assist Customs and the Immigration Departments were mobilised to provide all possible assistance.

The Italian nationals have already left the island in a chartered plane of the Italian carrier "Alitalia" which has taken them to Rome. As there were some spare seats on the plane a priority list as arranged so that special cases could leave promptly.

[The article above was accompanied by two photos of ships with the caption: Another 600 evacuees, men, women, and children, arrived at Larnaca from Lebanon, fleeing from the war-stricken country. In the top picture, the Italian naval vessel "Nave Carole" which carried 457 persons of whom some 100 were Italians and the others of various nationalities. Below, the Lebanese craft "Eddy" which landed 147 evacuees mostly Lebanese and foreign students.]

Letter #2 Christmas 1982

P.C. Gupta
TIFR
Bombay 400005

Dear Chuk

Seasons Greetings
and
Best wishes for a
Very Very Happy and
Prosperous New Year

Prakash

Letter #3

Dr. P.C. Gupta
Tata Institute of Fundamental Research
Homi Bhabha Road
Bombay 400005

May 2, 1983

Dear Chuk,

It was good to receive your thoughtful letter. After the recent events and especially today's news (rocket over ambassador's residence) things don't appear to be that stable but anyway I am scheduled to leave for Beirut to-morrow morning. I expect to return by 12th of June.

In July this year I expect to visit Canada and USA. I would be participating in the 5th World Conference on Smoking and Health, 10-15th July, Winniepeg [sic], and then I plan to visit some Universities to give seminar about our epidemiologic work on oral cancer and precancerous lesions, and exchange ideas. I hope to come down to Washington, D.C. I would certainly call you, and like to meet you, if possible.

Warmest regards.
Yours sincerely,

Prakesh (signature)
Prakesh C Gupta, Sc.D.
Dental Research Section

Letters from Jerius Khuri

Note: I kept up a correspondence with Jerius Khuri for about six years. Only two of his letters remain. His letters were postmarked from various places, mostly outside Lebanon. He would write a letter and wait for someone who was going to Europe and they would post the letter to me. The instability of the post in Lebanon was the reason for this.

In his last letter to me, he told me he was investigating the ministry as a new career.

Beirut, 8, March, 1983

Dear Chuck,

I was quite pleased to receive your letter and make sure you have been able to return safely to your family. To tell you the truth, I feared not how you would make it when you get to sea, but I was anxious about your crossing from West Beirut to Juniah under all the anti-aircraft shelling. Anyhow, thanks to God who has kept you and most of my friends plus myself and relatives by the bond of his love.

As for my news, it is quite usual. My work with the group of Mills and Boon goes on routinely. My studies are not hindered by my work, and I have been able to pass my first semester with a B score. Lebanon has been, and still is, hit by a snowstorm, that has not taken place in the country or the region for decades. My mountain village where my mother and sister live has been isolated by snowfall. Its thickness has reached a record this year, six feet and a few inches. Nobody in my village has been hurt by it, however.

I have to register my gratitude for your hospitality and

love, of which I am deeply confident and happy. In any case, I suppose I will not be coming to the States for study in the near future. But, I would think that I have a true friend there. Greetings to everyone in the family. May God bless you all and keep you in His grace.

I look forward to hear from you soon, and wish a merry Easter.

Yours sincerely, Jerius Khuri

The following letter was received January 25, 1988, although dated many months prior to that.

Lehfed, 29, September, 1987

Dear Chuck,

It has been a long time we did not correspond. I very much miss your news and letters. I hope everything is o.k. with you and the rest of the family.

I tell you that I have graduated a year ago with my Master's degree. I continue to work in translation and research, and I have contracts with more than one publishing house. My mother and sister are quite fine. Nothing is new with me save my progress in using the Optacon, an electronic device used to make the visually handicapped read the usual print. The only other exciting news is that I was planning to leave Lebanon for some time to work in one of the rich Gulf shiekdoms, but unfortunately the two places I contacted told me that they are not filling any vacancies because of the squeeze on expenses due to the long Iraqi-Iranian war.

What a lovely time one has thanking God for keeping him alive and well - provided in a country like Lebanon. Our currency has been depreciated by about ninety-seven percent in almost three years. Since the beginning of last June, the exchange value of the dollar against the Lebanese pound or lira has risen by about one hundred and thirty-five percent, i.e., on the first of June we used to pay one hundred and twenty pounds to buy a dollar. Today we pay two hundred and eighty pounds, on average, to buy a dollar. Diesel fuel is almost out of supply. If one finds it, one has to pay exactly twenty-five percent of the lowest minimum salary, or the equivalent of one thousand liras. Most of the Lebanese live in fear of not being warmed up by electric or diesel heaters in what appears to promise to be a long, severe winter. A high percentage of the Lebanese are unemployed or underemployed, and had not been for the four-time increase in the wages of daily labourers, many families would find themselves starving. This does not mean that people are having enough, nourishing meals every day.

Despite all this, I praise God because I still find some good work. True it is not well paid if compared with the rents paid three years ago, but it is earning some decent living.

I look forward to hear soon from you on everything, and hope you will use the address written on the envelop.

Sincerely yours, Jerius Khuri

WHERE ARE THEY NOW?

Luigi Cerofolini

Luigi was a professor from Bologna, Italy, and shared Marquand House for part of my time there. He left before the crisis of war. He gave me his address. I wrote him later, but never heard from him. I know nothing more of him.

Colin Newell

When we met, Colin and I shared Marquand House and then the great adventure. He was a young man, single, a demography graduate student at the London School of Hygiene and Tropical Medicine. I recall him telling me he was a native of Scotland. He had a girl friend named Marie-Louise, from the Netherlands.

I found him on April 8, 2005 by contacting the university where he studied in 1982. He wrote me these e-mails, in reply to my search.

E mail #1: (April 8, 2005) *The electronic bush-telegraph seems to be as efficient as ever! The long-serving postmaster at LSHTM (Many thanks, Margaret!) passed your message on to my wife, who still works in academia, close to LSHTM, and she has passed it on to me. Not bad - three steps in about four hours!*

I'm guessing that you are the person I shared a house with for a few days in American Univ of Beirut when the Israelis invaded in 1982, and we were evacuated by boat to Cyprus, but were diverted to Haifa where you arranged for the UK ambassador to fetch me off the boat. Am I correct?

I'm fine, working as a database administrator and web designer in an engineering company in south London, a job I've been in since 1988.

How about you? From your email it appears you've also left the academic world? And what is your book about?? How is your family?
Do let me know.
Best regards
Colin Newell

[I replied as follows immediately the same day.]

To: Colin Newell
Subject: Re: Greetings from London UK
This is amazing. I can't believe I found you so easily. I used to come to England a lot, and wish I had known you were there. When we met you were dating a lady named Marie-Louise from the Netherlands.

I cannot begin to tell you about my life these past 23 years - so very much has happened. I was divorced shortly after returning, and began to raise four daughters. Later I would raise foster kids and take in "strays" too, some 15 or more, many handicapped and international. I quit my world traveling until about 1990 when I went back to Egypt. By then I was a "well-known" guy and was recruited at the end of the Cold War in 1991 to help stabilize the Soviet Union through work with the State Department, the World Bank, and my university. I worked there for five years, coming and going, in Siberia, Ukraine, Russia, Kazakhstan, Uzbekistan, Turkmenistan, Georgia, etc. and loved the work. [By then my children were mostly grown and gone from home.] I continued work in Eastern Europe, being based in the Czech Republic until 1996. By then I was a full professor and director of International Development for the University here.

I hope you are sitting down for the rest of this! Then I sold my home, quit my job and entered seminary to become a Roman Catholic priest. I was ordained in May 2000 and am now pastor of Sacred Heart Catholic Church, Danville, VA, where I have been for three years.

I have a granddaughter now, aged 14 months. Life has been good and a bit complicated. But I am incredibly happy.

I have been asked to publish my memoirs of all my travels, and also my edited diary from Beirut trips. I am considering doing both. During my travels I have been caught in several revolutions and a coup-de-etat on Red Square in Moscow, I have been on a jumbo jet which caught fire at 42 thousand feet, and much more. Anyway, if I do the Beirut story, using my detailed diary for its base, I want to credit you, and tell where you now are.

So, your turn. What is up? In trying to find you, I did find a demography book circa 1990 by you. Right? Tell me all about yourself and what has happened to you.

Chuck Breindel

[Colin replied quickly by e mail the next day.]

Chuck,

Well, that is certainly a more interesting c.v. than mine!
Well, I married Marie-Louise in 1984, and we had two children, Nicolas and Anna, and they are 19 and 17 now. Anna is in first year at university studying geography & Development studies, having spent last year in a rural school in Tanzania teaching primary health matters - mainly HIV awareness/prevention. Nic is in his final year at school, and goes on to university later this year, to study engineering.

Marie-Louise is a professor of paediatric epidemiology here in London, whose main interest is the transmission on HIV from mother to child. - try Googling for Marie-Louise Newell.

Now that our kids have just about left school, we're suddenly feeling a bit less tied to our local area. Maybe we'll end up living in Africa - our favourite continent. We have been on several safaris in east and south Africa in recent years, and Marie-Louise has strong work contacts in Malawi and KwaZulu Natal.

My work, as you can guess, is pretty boring to outsiders, but I keep interested in the technology, and I do a fair amount of database development work in my spare time (sad, I know!)

Do try to write your Beirut story. It was a long time ago but I'm sure the memories will come back once you start.

Do keep in touch.   Colin

Prakesh Gupta
Prakesh C. Gupta was a visiting professor at AUB, and was working there before I arrived in late May. He was from Tata Institute of Fundamental Research, Bombay, India, where he did research on oral diseases. I never met him until the fateful day when we were being evacuated from AUB. Despite some correspondence for a year, I know nothing more of him.

Robert Norton
Bob Norton was a professor from Yarmuk University in northern Jordan. He taught in the discipline of Education there, and was at AUB to do some guest lecturing. He was a native of Utah in the United States. I did not know him at AUB but, like Prakesh Gupta, our fates intertwined at our evacuation and until Haifa, Israel. I wrote to him once, but heard nothing in reply. I do not know where he is or what happened to him.

President of AUB, David Dodge

David was acting president of the University, and had not yet arrived to assume his position when I got there. He came shortly thereafter, and we met again at Marquand House. I had met him earlier in Washington, D.C. when I was recruited to come to AUB earlier in 1982, I believe. On July 19, 1982 David Dodge was captured on his way back from his AUB office by Hizballah. He was held over a year and then released. He died shortly afterward, I was told.

Omar Faour

Mr. Faour was the wonderful driver from the car pool of AUB who helped me escape twice in one day. When he found out we had no money, he was concerned that we may have difficulty surviving in the East of Beirut. He gave us 300 pounds of his own money. I sent my half back to him once I got home. He was later killed in the ground fighting sometime in the early 1980's, I was informed. I cannot confirm this, however.

Dr. Nabil Kronfol

Nabil was chairman of Health Services Research, the department at AUB where I taught. He was my supervisor there. He was married and had two children, as I can recall. We continued to stay in touch for a while and, because of mutual friends, I knew he had gone from Lebanon to Saudi Arabia for a time, and then to the United States. My current knowledge is that he is back in Lebanon, continuing to develop Health Services Administration. I found him on the web in April 2005 and wrote to him. He replied twice:

Dear Chuck,
It is indeed a pleasure to hear from you after such a long time. I hope you are doing well.
I am pleased to have your contacts.
I am doing well thanks to God. I am still teaching, consulting, traveling, ... the usual kind of events !! I am attaching herewith my contacts.

Please send me yours as well.
Regards
Nabil M Kronfol MD, DrPHHealth Systems and Health Manpower
DevelopmentPresident
Lebanese HealthCare Management AssociationPOB 113-7400Beirut
- Lebanon

And the second reply came quickly:

Dear Charles,
 I am so pleased to hear from you. I did suspect that you had entered priesthood from your e-mail address (Friar or Father Charles). This is great. I also hope that our paths will meet again in Lebanon, the USA or in the region. I see that you have worked in Egypt. I wish we had remained in touch then. Cairo is a very frequent destination for me and has always been, because of the regional office of the World Health Organization. Thanks to God, I am still very active all over the region, as I mentioned in my message yesterday.
My daughter is now married in Houston. She is a physician (pediatrician) and married to yet another physician (a neurosurgeon). My younger son is in Med II with one more year to go at AUB.
My wife and I are busy also in charitable work in Lebanon.
Let us keep in touch. send me your telephone numbers and your address Nabil M Kronfol MD, DrPH.

Haroutune Armenian, MD, Dr.PH.

Dr. Armenian was dean of the Faculty of Public Health when I was there. He had a wife and two young children, and lived within the AUB compound in faculty housing. He left Lebanon and continued a very successful career in Baltimore Maryland at Johns Hopkins University. He is there to this day.

Dr. Nadim Karam

Nadim was a young physician who taught in the same department with me. He befriended me on an earlier visit to AUB. During my stay he provided me with warmth, recreation, and professional collegiality. His wife was also a physician. They opened a clinic in the mountain resort town of Brummana that fateful June. They had three children, twins and a little girl, all born on the same day, but one year apart.

Just one quick search of the web, and I found him. He wrote back this reply:

March 29, 2005: It is great to hear from you; one more miracle of the Internet. You guessed right. Your memory is great; actually I was recently (the past month or so) talking to colleagues about your adventure in Lebanon and the little adventure as we crossed check points. Huda and I remember your visit very well. I always wondered where you were. I hope all is well with you and your family. Let me brief you about us: We are still in Lebanon and in Brummana. I left AUB to join the University of Balamand (I am Dean of Health Sciences and Vice President). I continue to operate my clinic in Brummana in the evening. And, among other things, I direct WRF. Our three kids are doing well; they are in the US. The boy and girl twins are doing graduate work at MIT. Zahi (boy) is in electrical engineering and Hanan (girl) is in Hydrology; both are finishing their Master's degree on a PhD track. Samer, the younger is at NJIT (New Jersey) finishing his Master (this month) in IT. He is not sure if he wants to pursue a Ph.D. immediately and is interested in joining the industry.
Let me hear your news. All the Best. Nadim

Karen Hajj

Karen was a student from Pennsylvania studying at AUB. I met here on the S.S Edy when we were thrown together for a few difficult days. She has some Lebanese ancestry, she told me, and that was the attraction to study in Beirut. After we were back home, there was some brief correspondence, and a phone call each way. She had done some media program, a morning show, and took much abuse for it because her story was not substantiated by other news available here. I don't know where she is.

James Brown, III

As the American consul to Israel, he lived with his wife in Tel Aviv. We met in a warehouse in the port of Haifa. We spent the next 36 hours as colleagues. He arranged for me and Karen Hajj to stay in Tel Aviv a day, so that an attache could come from D.C. to interrogate us about what was really happening in Beirut. We were the first and, to that point, only ones to get out. He was a large bearded and jolly fellow. His son was there from the USA at that time. I recall that the son was a student at the University of Virginia, so near to my own home in Virginia. He gave me two Jerusalem pottery mugs from his office there. I have them in my den to this day, and treasure them.

I contacted the Tel Aviv embassy in April 2005, in an effort to locate Mr. Brown. I got this reply:

04:39PM April 12, 2005

Sorry, he is no longer at Post and no one has a forwarding address. You might try the State Department website.

                     U.S. Embassy, Israel, Web Team

Pete Peterson

Mr. Peterson, whom I recall being called "Captain Peterson," accompanied Mr. Brown to the port in Haifa and seemed to be doing a lot of work to get us out of there. He told me that Secretary of State Alexander Haig learned of our situation and there had been much activity in Washington to communicate with Israel for a couple of days, in order to get us free. I had the impression that I owed a lot to him personally. He came to the port with a wife. He was trim and attractive in appearance, that is, he was warm and welcoming, with no airs about him.

BIOGRAPHICAL SKETCH: Rev. Charles L. Breindel, Ph.D., is pastor of Sacred Heart Roman Catholic Church, in Danville, Virginia. He was ordained as a priest for the Diocese of Richmond on May 27, 2000. He completed his studies for the priesthood at Catholic University of America, Washington, DC, and lived in seminary formation at Theological College while doing his studies.

A native of St. Marys, Pennsylvania, he was born in 1948. He attended state universities in Pennsylvania, earning a B.S. summa cum laude, M.S., M.A., and Ph.D. prior to his work in health care planning and management.

Prior to entering seminary in 1996, he was director of international development for Virginia Commonwealth University, and Professor of Health Administration, Medical College of Virginia, Richmond Virginia. He has traveled extensively throughout the world, assisting the World Bank, the United States and many other countries in development, particularly in the Middle East and the countries of the former Soviet Union. He has published more than sixty articles, monographs, and book chapters.

He has held executive positions in hospitals, health systems and university. He was also in senior consulting with Arthur Young and Company and Ernst & Young. He has served on many regional, state, and national committees and commissions as well.

On a personal level, he has four grown daughters, one grand-daughter, and has also raised three foster sons. When he can find free time, he enjoys running, mountain hiking, reading, and singing.

His earlier book mentioned herein is **Born in Beirut: A Priesthood**, Danville, VA: CL Breindel LLC, 2005. It is available at www.sheartcatholic.com.